Stage 2 Paper 8

Business and Company Law

First edition 1996
Fourth edition January 1999

ISBN 0 7517 3477 2 (previous edition 0 7517 3447 0)

British Library Cataloguing-in-Publication Data

A catalogue record for this book
is available from the British Library

Published by

BPP Publishing Limited
Aldine House, Aldine Place
London W12 8AW

http://www.bpp.co.uk

Printed in Great Britain by Ashford Colour Press, Gosport, Hants.

If you use CIMA **Passcards**, you can be sure that the time you spend on final revision for your **1999 exams** is time well spent.

- They **save you time**: following the structure of the BPP Study Text for Paper 8, important facts on key exam topics are summarised for you

- They incorporate diagrams to kick start your memory

- They are pocket-sized: you can run through them **anytime** and **anywhere**

CIMA **Passcards** focus on the exam you will be facing.

- They highlight which topics have been examined - and when

- They provide you with suggestions on subject examinability, given past exams and the direction the examiner appears to be taking, in **exam focus points**

- They give you useful **exam hints** that can earn you those vital extra marks in the exam

Run through the complete set of **Passcards** as often as you can during your final revision period. The day before the exam, try to go through the **Passcards** again. You will then be well on your way to passing your exams. **Good luck!**

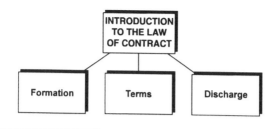

Note. This chapter provides a very brief overview of the material contained in **Chapters 1-6**.

Formation

A contract may be defined as an agreement which legally binds the parties. The courts usually look for the evidence of three essential elements in any contract.

- There is an agreement made by *offer* and *acceptance*

- There is a bargain by which the obligations assumed by each party are supported by *consideration* given by the other

- The parties must have an *intention to create legal relations* between themselves

Even if these essential elements can be shown, validity may be affected by the following.

- Some persons have only restricted *capacity* to contract
- Some contracts must be made in a particular *form*

Terms

As a general principle the parties to a contract may, by their offer and acceptance, include in their contract whatever terms they prefer. Terms may be express or implied.

- One party may seek to incorporate a particular type of term which excludes his liability for negligence or breach of contract. This is the *exclusion clause*

- Statements made in pre-contract negotiations may become terms of the contract or may remain representations. If a representation turns out to be untrue, the party misled may have a remedy for *misrepresentation*

Discharge

Most contracts come to an end when both parties have fulfilled or performed their contractual obligations. There are, however, other ways in which a contract may be discharged, including breach of contract.

A number of *remedies* are available for breach of contract.

- Damages is the most usual common law remedy

- Equitable remedies may be available in certain circumstances

Exam focus. Do not neglect the latter areas of contract law. Topics like frustration and remoteness and measure of damages are examined regularly.

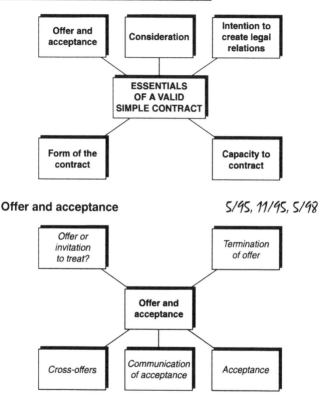

Offer and acceptance

5/95, 11/95, 5/98

Offer or invitation to treat?

An offer is a definite promise to be bound on specific terms. It cannot be vague, but can be made certain by reference to previous dealings.

- *Gunthing v Lynn 1831*
- *Hillas & Co Ltd v Arcos Ltd 1932*

It does not need to be made to a specific person.

- *Carlill v Carbolic Smoke Ball Co 1893*

Only an offer made with the intention that it shall be binding when accepted may be accepted so as to form a binding contract. A response to a request for information is not necessarily an offer.

- *Bigg v Boyd Gibbons 1971*
- *Harvey v Facey 1893*

A 'promise' may be construed as a binding offer if unclear

- *Bowerman v ABTA 1996*

An *invitation to treat* occurs where a party is initiating negotiations or inviting another party to make an offer. It cannot be accepted to form a binding contract. Four categories can be identified.

- Auction sales: the bid equates to an offer, which the auctioneer may accept or reject
  - *Payne v Cave 1789*

- An advertisement in a newspaper or journal is an attempt to induce offers which is not itself an offer
  - *Partridge v Crittenden 1968*

- An exhibition of goods for sale, such as the display of goods in a shop window, or the placing of goods on shelves in a self-service shop, is not an offer
  - *Fisher v Bell 1961*

- o *Pharmaceutical Society of Great Britain v Boots Cash Chemists (Southern) 1952*

- An invitation for tenders does not amount to an offer. The tender itself is the offer.

Termination of offer

An offer may only be accepted while it is still open. It may be terminated so that it is no longer open for acceptance.

A rejection by the offeree terminates the offer. This may be outright rejection or a counter-offer, which is also a rejection of the original offer.

- *Hyde v Wrench 1840*

Lapse of time may also terminate an offer. An offer expires after a reasonable time if no express time limit is set. What is reasonable depends on circumstances.

- *Ramsgate Victoria Hotel Co v Montefiore 1866*

Revocation by the offeror terminates the offer. The offer may be revoked at any time before acceptance.

- *Payne v Cave 1789*

- Offeror is only bound to keep offer open if bound to do so by separate contract (with separate consideration)
  - o *Routledge v Grant 1828*

- Revocation must be communicated
  - o *Byrne v Van Tienhoven 1880*

- Revocation may be communicated via a third party
  - o *Dickinson v Dodds 1876*

An offer may be conditional. Failure of a condition means offer cannot be accepted.

- *Financings Ltd v Stimson 1962*

Death of the offeree terminates the offer. Death of the offeror terminates the offer unless the offer is accepted in ignorance of offeror's death and the offer is not of a personal nature.

- *Bradbury v Morgan 1862*

Acceptance

This must be unqualified agreement to the terms of the offer.

- May be by words, may be by action, as in *Carlill*, or may be inferred from conduct
  - *Brogden v Metropolitan Railway Co 1877*
- May not be inferred from silence
  - *Felthouse v Bindley 1862*
- May be acceptance by offeror of a counter-offer: counter-offer is a final rejection of original offer and itself constitutes a new offer
  - *Butler Machine Tool Co v Ex-Cell-O Corp (England) 1979*
- A request for information in response to an offer is neither acceptance nor rejection
  - *Stevenson v McLean 1880*

Exam focus. 'Requests for information' was specifically examined in Section B of the May 1998 paper.

- Acceptance 'subject to contract' does not bind (eg in contracts for sale and purchase of land)

Communication of acceptance

General rule: acceptance must be communicated to the offeror and is not effective until this has been done. There are two exceptions to this.

- The offeror may dispense with (waive) the need for communication of acceptance
  - *Carlill v Carbolic Smoke Ball Co 1893*

- The postal rule: where the use of the post is within the contemplation of both parties, acceptance is complete and effective as soon as a letter is posted
  - *Adams v Lindsell 1818*
  - *Household Fire and Carriage Accident Insurance Co v Grant 1879*

In the case of instantaneous communications such as telex, fax or the Internet, acceptance must be understood.

- *Entores v Miles Far Eastern Corporation 1955*

For a prescribed mode of acceptance to be mandatory, it must be very precisely requested, otherwise any equally expeditious method will suffice.

- *Yates Building Co v R J Pulleyn & Sons (York) 1975*

- Example: 'notice in writing' means notice received by offeror
  - *Holwell Securities v Hughes 1974*

Acceptance may only be made by an authorised person: this means the offeree or his authorised agent.

- *Powell v Lee 1908*

Cross-offers

If two offers identical in terms cross in the post, there is no contract, as there has been no acceptance.

- *Tinn v Hoffmann 1873*

Exam focus. Acceptance is already looking like a hot topic, with the examiner presenting 'hypothetical but realistic' scenarios involving communication of acceptance on a regular basis.

Consideration   5/95, 5/97

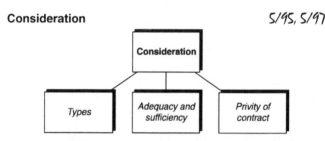

There are two useful case law definitions of consideration.

- A valuable consideration in the sense of the law may consist either in some right, interest, profit or benefit accruing to one party, or some forbearance, detriment, loss or responsibility given, suffered or undertaken by the other
  - *Currie v Misa 1875*

- An act or forbearance of one party, or the promise thereof, is the price for which the promise of the other is bought, and the promise thus given for value is enforceable
  - *Dunlop v Selfridge 1915*

Types

Consideration may be executed or executory, but it may not be past.

Executed: an act in return for a promise.

- Example: placing an order for goods and paying for them at the time the order is placed

Executory: a promise in return for a promise.

- Example: placing an order for goods and agreeing to pay within 30 days of delivery

Past: something which has already been done before a promise is given in return. This is, as a rule, not sufficient to make the promise binding.

- Examples
  - *Re McArdle 1951*
  - *Roscorla v Thomas 1842*
- Exceptions
  - S 27 Bills of Exchange Act 1882
  - Debts statute-barred under Limitation Act 1980
  - Request for services implying promise to pay
    - *Lampleigh v Braithwait 1615*

Adequacy and sufficiency

The courts will not enquire into *adequacy* of consideration. There is no remedy at law for someone who simply makes a bad bargain.

- *Thomas v Thomas 1842*

Consideration must be *sufficient*. Consideration is sufficient if it has some identifiable value.

- *Chappell & Co v Nestlé 1960*

Various questions arise in respect of sufficiency of performance of existing duties.

- Performance of existing duties *imposed by statute* is no consideration
  o *Collins v Godefroy 1831*
  o Unless extra service is given
    - *Glasbrook Bros v Glamorgan CC 1925*

- Performance of existing duties *under a contract* is no consideration for promise of additional reward
  o *Stilk v Myrick 1809*
  o Unless more than existing duties provided
    - *Hartley v Ponsonby 1857*
  o Where both parties derive benefit, courts may uphold additional promise, provided no duress or fraud
    - *Williams v Roffey Bros & Nicholls (Contractors) Ltd 1990*

Exam focus. In May 1997 the issue arose as to whether carrying out an existing obligation may be contractural consideration.

- *Waiver of existing rights*: part payment of debt in full settlement is insufficient consideration to make waiver binding. Consideration must be provided if the waiver is to be binding
  o *Foakes v Beer 1884*

- o Exceptions are as follows
  - – Goods instead of cash
  - – Early settlement
    Pinnel's case 1602
  - – Settlement with several creditors
  - – Payment by third party
  - – Principle of promissory estoppel

Principle of promissory estoppel provides that, if a waiver is given with the intention that the debtor should act on it and the debtor does so, creditor may be estopped from retracting his promise.

- *Central London Property Trust v High Trees House 1947*

- This is a shield not a sword
  - o *Combe v Combe 1951*

- The promise of waiver must be entirely voluntary
  - o *D and C Builders v Rees 1966*

Exam focus. The case of *Williams v Roffey Bros* remains important, but you must be aware of the exceptions to it.

Privity of contract   *11/98*

There is a rule that consideration must move from the promisee.

- *Tweddle v Atkinson 1861*

Developed from this is the doctrine of privity of contract. Only a person who is a party to a contract has enforceable rights or obligations under it.

- *Dunlop v Selfridge 1915*

- *Beswick v Beswick 1968*

There are a number of exceptions to the doctrine of privity of contract.

- Statutory exceptions, such as the Road Traffic Act 1972 and the Married Woman's Property Act 1882

- Doctrine of undisclosed principal

- Restrictive covenant which runs with land
  - *Tulk v Moxhay 1848*

- Collateral contracts
  - *Shanklin Pier Ltd v Detel Products 1951*

- The rights contained in a contract may be formally assigned. The assignment must be absolute, in writing and notice must be given to the other party

Intention to create legal relations

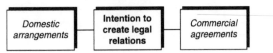

There may be an express statement of intention or otherwise. This is usually conclusive. If there is no express statement, two rebuttable presumptions may be applied.

Domestic arrangements

In domestic arrangements, it is presumed that there is *no* intention to create legal relations.

- Husband and wife

- o Non-separated
    - – *Balfour v Balfour 1919*
- o Separated: more likely that intention will be inferred
    - – *Merritt v Merritt 1970*
- Other arrangements: an intention may be inferred if there is 'mutuality' in the arrangements
    - o *Simpkins v Pays 1955*

Commercial agreements

In commercial agreements, it is presumed that there *is* an intention to create legal relations.

- May be expressly disclaimed as, for example, 'not subject to legal jurisdiction'
    - o *Rose and Frank v Crompton 1923*
- Burden of proof is on party seeking to escape liability
    - o *Edwards v Skyways Ltd 1964*
- 'Comfort letters' impose moral obligations only
    - o *Kleinwort Benson Ltd v Malaysia Mining Corporation Bhd 1989*

Capacity to contract

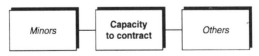

Minors

Position is determined by Minors' Contracts Act 1987.

Valid contracts are binding on the minor.

- A contract for supply of goods and services which are necessaries is valid
  - *Suitability* is measured by living standards of the minor
  - *Needs* relate to personal requirements of minor
  - Goods for use in a trade are not necessaries, nor are goods with which minor is already well supplied
    - *Nash v Inman 1908*
    - *Mercantile Union Guarantee Corpn v Ball 1937*

- A service contract for the minor's benefit is valid
  - *Doyle v White City Stadium 1935*
  - *Chaplin v Leslie Frewin (Publishers) Ltd 1966*

Voidable contracts are certain contracts by which a minor acquires an interest of a continuing nature, for example, leases, purchase of shares or a partnership agreement.

- Voidable during minority and within reasonable time after majority

- Rescission relieves minor of future obligations

- Must rescind within reasonable time of majority
  - *Edwards v Carter 1893*

All other contracts entered into by a minor are *unenforceable*. The minor is not bound, but the other party is. To be bound, the minor must ratify within reasonable time of majority.

Others

Companies do not have the same capacity as individuals, as they are 'artificial' legal persons. Actions outside powers granted by constitution are *ultra vires*. This is of limited effect since CA 1989.

Persons who are *mentally incapacitated* are bound unless

- Incapable of understanding nature of contract
- The other party knows or ought to know of incapacity

Form of the contract

Some rights and obligations are only binding if in the form of a *deed*.

- Prior to LoP(MP)A 1989, a seal was required
- Deed must be in writing, signed and 'delivered'
- Examples
  - Lease for 3 years or more
  - Promise not supported by consideration

Some commercial contracts are void unless *in writing*.

- Examples
  - Transfer of shares
  - Consumer credit contracts

Some contracts may be made orally, but must be *evidenced in writing* to be enforceable.

- Most important is contract of guarantee
- Signed note of material terms will suffice

Special considerations apply to business conducted on-line. The law is in its infancy. The following questions are to be resolved.

- Can a contract be said to be in writing? (Probably, yes)
- Is it signed?
- When is an offer accepted?

- Are there problems with payment (consideration)?

> *Exam focus.* Form is more likely to feature in MCQs than in an essay question, as the depth of knowledge required here is not very great. If you get a question on the electronic contract, apply ordinary principles of contract law and use common sense.

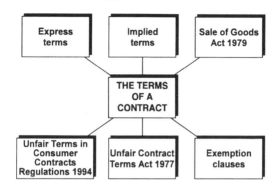

Express terms   *11/95*

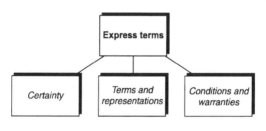

Certainty

A legally binding agreement must be certain in its terms. If it is impossible to identify a contract from the language used, the courts will hold that there is no contract.

- *Scammell v Ouston 1941*

Parties may leave a term to be settled by specified means outside the contract. Example: open market price on day of delivery.

Terms may be determined by course of dealing between parties.

- *Hillas & Co Ltd v Arcos Ltd 1932*

Terms and representations

May be necessary to decide whether words amount to a contract term or are merely a representation, ie something which induces formation of a contract but which does not become a contract term.

- Courts may look at timing of representation
  - *Bannerman v White 1861*
  - *Routledge v McKay 1954*

- If party has special knowledge of subject, it is more likely to be contract term
  - *Dick Bentley Productions v Arnold Smith Motors 1965*
  - *Oscar Chess v Williams 1957*

Conditions and warranties

Terms can be classified as conditions or warranties.

A *condition* is a vital term going to the root of the contract. Breach entitles injured party to treat the contract as discharged and claim damages.

- *Poussard v Spiers 1876*

A *warranty* is a term subsidiary to the main purpose of the contract. Breach entitles injured party to claim damages only.

- *Bettini v Gye 1876*

The courts may look at effect of breach to determine how term should be classified. If this is not clear, then it may be identified as an innominate term.

- *Hong Kong Fir Shipping Co Ltd v Kawasaki Kisa Kaisha Ltd 1962*

Exam focus. Part (a) of the Nov 1995 question on contract terms referred to 'breach of contract' rather than 'breach of contractual terms'. As the part (b) scenario showed, though, it was in fact a question primarily on contract terms. You will sometimes find that part (b) of a question tests your ability to apply knowledge already demonstrated in part (a) to a scenario and this has been the pattern for question 2 in both papers so far.

Implied terms   11/96

Term may be implied by trade *custom* or practice.

- *Hutton v Warren 1836*

- Express term may overrule custom
  - *Les Affreteurs v Walford 1919*

Terms may be implied by *statute*.

- Some statutory terms may be excluded, for example, the Partnership Act 1890

- Some are obligatory, for example those implied by ss 12-15 Sale of Goods Act 1979

Terms may be implied by the *courts* to give the contract 'business efficacy'.

- *The Moorcock 1889*

- *Liverpool City Council v Irwin 1977*

Sale of Goods Act 1979   11/96

The definition of a consumer is important. A party to a contract 'deals as a consumer' in the following circumstances.

- He does not make contract in course of business

- The other party does make contract in course of business

- In a sale of goods contract, goods are of type ordinarily supplied for private use or consumption
  o S 12, UCTA 1977

Key implied terms are contained in ss 12-15 of SGA 1979.

- Section 12: title
  o Implied condition that seller has a right to sell the goods
  o Implied warranties
    – Goods free from charge or encumbrance not disclosed
    – Buyer will enjoy quiet possession
  o *Niblett v Confectioners Materials 1921*

- Section 13: description
  o Implied condition that goods correspond with the description
  o *Beale v Taylor 1967*

- Section 14(2): satisfactory quality
  o Goods must meet the standard that a reasonable person would regard as satisfactory
  o Replaces merchantable quality provision
  o Goods must now be fit for all purposes for which commonly bought

- Section 14(3): fitness for purpose
  o Implied condition that goods are reasonably fit for buyer's disclosed purpose

- o Disclosure may be express or implied
  - – *Priest v Last 1903*

- Section 15: sale by sample
  - o Implied condition that bulk will correspond with sample in quality

Exclusion clauses   *11/97, 5/98, 11/98*

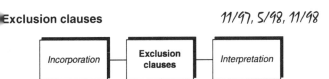

Incorporation

Any term, including exclusion clauses, must be properly incorporated into a contract. Case law rules are as follows.

- Document containing notice of clause must be an integral part of the contract
  - o *Chapelton v Barry UDC 1940*
  - o *Thompson v LMS Railway 1930*

- If document signed, clause usually binding
  - o *L'Estrange v Graucob 1934*
  - o Not if misleading explanation given
    - – *Curtis v Chemical Cleaning Co 1951*

- Terms must be put forward before contract made
  - o *Olley v Marlborough Court 1949*
  - o *Thornton v Shoe Lane Parking Ltd 1971*
  - o Unless consistent with previous dealings
    - – *J Spurling Ltd v Bradshaw 1956*
    - – *Hollier v Rambler Motors 1972*

- Onerous terms must be sufficiently highlighted
  - *Interfoto Picture Library Ltd v Stiletto Visua Programmes Ltd 1988*

Interpretation

Courts will interpret any ambiguity against the person seekin to rely on the exclusion clause (*contra proferentem*).

- *Hollier v Rambler Motors 1972*

If negligence is to be covered, this must be clear.

- *Alderslade v Hendon Laundry 1945*

Exam focus. In November 1997 you were asked to explain the extent to which professionals may exclude liability for negligence by relying on an exclusion clause.

Unfair Contract Terms Act 1977

UCTA applies to clauses inserted into contracts b commercial concerns or businesses.

- Any clause purporting to restrict liability for death c personal injury resulting from negligence is void

- Any clause purporting to restrict liability for own breach c contract is void unless the term is reasonable
  - Where using standard terms of business
  - Where other party deals as consumer

In sale of goods contracts, terms:

- Cannot, in any contract, restrict implied condition as to titl

- Cannot, in consumer contract, restrict the statutory implied terms in ss 13-15

- Where buyer not dealing as consumer, ss 13-15 may be restricted if this satisfies test of reasonableness

Other clauses will be upheld if they are reasonable under s 11. A range of factors has to be considered

- *St Albans City and District Council v International Computers Ltd 1994*

Unfair Terms in Consumer Contracts Regulations 1994

These regulations, which supplement common law and UCTA, apply to consumer contracts in which contractual terms have not been individually negotiated.

- Unfair terms: contrary to requirements of good faith causes imbalance in rights and obligations to detriment of consumer

- Terms should be written in clear intelligible language; if unclear, construed against seller

Two types of redress are available

- Consumer can ask court to find that unfair term should not be binding
- Complaint can be made to DGFT, who can seek injunction against unfair term

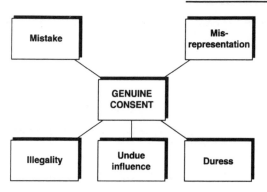

Mistake

There are three categories of operative mistake. Only in restricted circumstances will any type of mistake render a contract void.

Common mistake occurs where both parties contract under the same misapprehension.

- *Res extincta:* the subject matter does not exist
  - *Couturier v Hastie 1852*

- *Res sua:* the subject matter already belongs to the buyer
  - *Cochrane v Willis 1865*

The law on common mistake has been clarified. In particular the law is there to uphold rather than destroy agreements

- *Associated Japanese Bank (International) v Credit du Nord SA 1988*

Mutual mistake occurs where the parties are at cross purposes but neither realises it.

- *Raffles v Wichelhaus 1864*

However, usually the terms of the contact will resolve the misunderstanding.

- *Tamplin v James 1880*

Unilateral mistake occurs where one party is mistaken and the other party is aware of it. This may occur following a misrepresentation. Contract may be voidable for misrepresentation or void for mistake. The distinction determines who bears the loss.

Most cases of unilateral mistake involve mistake of identity:

- Non face-to-face
  - o If fraudulent adoption of identity of person known to seller, contract is void
    - *Cundy v Lindsay 1878*
  - o If alias is non-existent person, voidable for misrepresentation
    - *King's Norton Metal Co v Edridge Merrett & Co 1897*

- Face-to-face
  - o Usually no mistake of identity, so voidable for misrepresentation
    - *Phillips v Brookes 1919 and Lewis v Averay 1971*
  - o Exceptional decision in *Ingram v Little 1961*

Non est factum involves mistakes over documents.

- Must be a fundamental difference between legal effect of document signed and that intended by signatory

- Must be no carelessness on part of signatory
  - o *Saunders v Anglia Building Society 1971*

There are various reliefs for mistake. *Recission* may be claimed where contract is voidable (see below: **Misrepresentation**). *Rectification* may be claimed where parties had a 'common intention' and the document does not correctly express their common intention.

* *Joscelyne v Nissen 1970*

There may also be one-off equitable remedies available.

The courts may impose a compromise.

* *Solle v Butcher 1950*

Courts may refuse an order for specific performance.

* *Webster v Cecil 1861*

Misrepresentation   *5/95, 5/96*

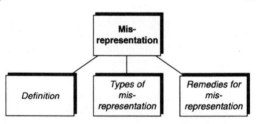

Definition

A misrepresentation can be defined as follows.

* A representation of fact which is untrue

* Made by one party to the other before the contract is made

* An inducement to the party misled actually to enter into the contract

A statement of fact is a representation.

- A statement of opinion is not
  - *Bisset v Wilkinson 1927*

- A statement of intention is not
  - *Maddison v Alderson 1883*

- A statement of law is not

Silence does not constitute a representation, with three exceptions

- A half-truth can be false
  - *R v Kylsant 1931*

- Duty to correct a statement, true when made, which has become false
  - *With v O'Flanagan 1936*

- Contracts *uberrimae fidei*, such as contracts of insurance

The representation must have induced the person to enter into the contract. If there is no reliance on it by the other party, the action will fail.

Where unaware of misrepresentation
  - *Horsfall v Thomas 1862*

Where aware, but not influenced by it
  - *Smith v Chadwick 1884*

The other party is entitled to rely without making enquiries.

Redgrave v Hurd 1881

Types of misrepresentation

A *fraudulent* misrepresentation is a statement made with knowledge that it is untrue, or without believing it to be true, or recklessly, careless whether it be true or false. An absence of honest belief characterises this.

* *Derry v Peek 1889*

There are two approaches to *negligent* misrepresentation. Under the common law, it involves breach of a duty of care.

* *Hedley Byrne & Co Ltd v Heller & Partners Ltd 1963*

Liability depends upon existence of a special relationship. This can be inferred where the statement is made in some specialist or expert capacity.

* *Esso Petroleum Co v Mardon 1976*

The second approach is set out in the Misrepresentation Act 1967. Here, the burden of proof is on the representor to disprove negligence. It may be more advantageous to bring an action under the Act than at common law.

* *Howard Marine and Dredging Co Ltd v A Ogden & Sons (Excavations) Ltd 1978*

An *innocent* misrepresentation is any misrepresentation made without fault.

Exam focus. The legal effects of a misrepresentation have been examined in MCQs in both 1995 papers. In May 1996 misrepresentation featured in a problem question. You had to consider all the circumstances of the case, and the answer was by no means clear cut.

Remedies for misrepresentation

The effect of a misrepresentation is to make a contract *voidable,* ie valid unless set aside. Representee may affirm or rescind. May also be right to damages instead of, or as well as, rescission.

Rescission is an equitable right, by which the contract is set aside as if never entered into (terminated *ab initio*).

The right to rescind is lost in the following circumstances.

- If contract affirmed
  - *Long v Lloyd 1958*

- If parties cannot be restored to pre-contract position
  - *Clark v Dickson 1858*

- If position of third parties would be prejudiced
  - *White v Garden 1851*

- Lapse of time
  - *Leaf v International Galleries 1950*

Damages may be available, as follows.

- Fraudulent misrepresentation
  - In addition to, or instead of, rescission
  - Common law action for the tort of deceit

- Negligent misrepresentation
  - 1967 Act
  - Action at common law

- Innocent misrepresentation
  - Damages in lieu of rescission

Exam focus. A problem question on misrepresentation appeared in the May 1996 paper.

Duress   *5/95, 11/97*

A person induced to contract through duress is entitled to avoid it at common law. The contract is voidable because there is a lack of genuine consent.

- Duress is fundamentally a threat, typically of physical violence or imprisonment
  - *Cumming v Ince 1847*

- May be also threatened seizure of goods or property, termed 'economic duress'
  - *The Atlantic Baron 1979*
  - *Atlas Express Ltd v Kafco (Exporters and Distributors) Ltd 1989*

Undue influence   *11/97*

A person induced to contract through undue influence is entitled to avoid it. The contract is voidable because there is a lack of genuine consent.

For a claim to succeed, a relationship of *trust and confidence* must first be shown.

- May be assumed in certain instances, for example parent and minor child, trustee and beneficiary, doctor and patient

- There is a presumption that it does not exist in others, for example bank and customer, husband and wife

- The presumption can be rebutted and undue influence shown to exist
  - *William v Bayley 1866*

If it appears that there is undue influence, the party deemed stronger may resist claim by showing that weaker party did in fact exercise *free judgement*. This could be done by showing that an independent adviser was used.

- *Inche Noriah v Shaik Allie Bin Omar 1929*

- *Lloyds Bank v Bundy 1975*

The transaction will only be set aside if it can be shown that it is to the *manifest disadvantage* of the weaker party.

- If transaction is an ordinary business transaction, it may be upheld by court
  - *National Westminster Bank v Morgan 1985*

- If weaker party has obtained benefit from transaction, court may uphold it
  - *Bank of Credit and Commerce International v Aboody 1988*

Right to rescind may be lost in certain circumstances (see above: **Misrepresentation**). Even where undue influence shown, the right to rescind may be lost.

- *Allcard v Skinner 1887*

> *Exam focus.* Undue influence was examined, both in essay and in problem form, for the first time in November 1997.

Illegality 5/97

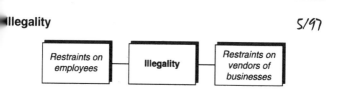

Any restriction on a person's normal freedom to carry on a trade, business or profession in such a way and with such persons as he chooses is a restraint of trade. A restraint of trade is void unless it can be justified.

- Person imposing restraint must have legitimate interest to protect

- Restraint must be reasonable between parties as a protection of that interest

- Restraint must be reasonable from the standpoint of the community
  - *Nordenfeldt v Maxim Nordenfeldt Guns and Ammunition Co 1894*

Restraints on employees

Such a restraint may, if reasonable in its extent, be valid if imposed to protect trade secrets or similar.

- Secret manufacturing processes can be protected
  - *Forster & Sons v Suggett 1918*

- Not personal skills acquired during employment
  - *Morris v Saxelby 1916*

Must also show that clause is reasonable between the parties, ie no more than is necessary to protect employer's interests.

- Local area can be protected
  - *Fitch v Dewes 1921*

- Wider range of activities cannot
  - *Attwood v Lamont 1920*
  - *Dawnay Day v D'Alphen 1997*

- If restraint too wide, whole restriction usually void

  o *Office Angels Ltd v Rainer-Thomas and O'Connor 1991*

  o Blue pencil rule may permit certain words only to be deleted

    – *Home Counties Dairies v Skilton 1970*

Restraints on vendors of businesses

Purchaser can protect what he has bought by imposing restrictions on vendor. Restraint must protect business sold, and must not be excessive.

- *British Reinforced Concrete Engineering Co v Schelff 1921*

For goodwill to be protected it must actually exist.

- *Vancouver Malt & Sake Brewing Co Ltd v Vancouver Breweries Ltd 1934*

> *Exam focus.* In May 1997 you were asked to explain the extent to which the law permits the use of contracts in restraint of trade to protect commercial interests. In part (b) of the same question, you had to apply the law to a problem.

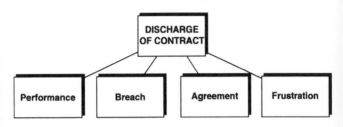

Performance   *11/97*

This is the normal method of discharge. Obligations are only discharged by complete and exact performance.

- *Cutter v Powell 1795*

There are exceptions to the rule.

- Substantial performance, eg building work
  - *Hoenig v Isaacs 1952*
- Acceptance of partial performance
  - *Sumpter v Hedges 1898*
- Prevention by the promisee of performance
  - *Planché v Colburn 1831*
- Performance by instalments of a divisible (severable) contract
  - *Taylor v Laird 1856*

> *Exam focus.* Discharge by performance was tested in problem form in November 1997.

Breach

A party, without lawful excuse, does not perform his contractual obligations precisely. Breach is an indication, by words or conduct, that he does not intend to honour his contractual obligations (repudiatory breach). The contract is not automatically discharged.

- Injured party may affirm the contract
  - _White & Carter (Councils) v McGregor 1961_

- Injured party may treat contract as repudiated by the other, recover damages and treat self as discharged from contractual obligations

Anticipatory breach is a type of breach. One party may declare in advance that will not perform when time for performance arrives.

- _Hochster v De La Tour 1853_

The other party may treat this as anticipatory breach and has two options.

- Treat the contract as discharged forthwith
- Allow the contract to continue until actual breach

There are risks where injured party allows contract to continue. The other party may change his mind and perform, or the parties may be discharged from obligations without liability by some other cause.

- _Avery v Bowden 1855_

Exam focus. Breach is always a popular exam topic as there are a number of aspects and effects which can be tested. In a scenario question, you should also consider whether one of the parties might try to plead frustration as an excuse for breach.

Agreement

Since a contract is created by agreement, it may be discharged by agreement. Agreement to cancel is a new contract for which consideration must be given.

- Novation: the parties enter into new contract, which provides necessary consideration

- Accord and satisfaction: one party has performed obligations and releases other from his obligations, eg by payment of a cancellation fee

Frustration   5/96

The doctrine

If it appears that the parties assumed that certain underlying conditions would continue and their assumption proves to be false, the contract may be frustrated. Examples are as follows.

- Destruction of subject matter
  - *Taylor v Caldwell 1863*

- Personal incapacity to render a contract of personal service
  - *Condor v Barron Knights 1966*

- Government intervention
  - *Metropolitan Water Board v Dick, Kerr & Co 1918*

- Supervening illegality
  - *Re Shipton, Anderson & Co and Harrison Bros & Co 1915*

- Non-occurrence of an event which is the sole purpose of the contract
  - *Krell v Henry 1903*
  - But where other purposes possible, courts will uphold contract
    - *Herne Bay Steamboat Co v Hutton 1903*
    - 'Coronation cases'

- Interruption which prevents performance in the form intended by the parties
  - *Jackson v Union Marine Insurance Co 1874*
  - *Gamerco SA v ICM 1995*

There is no discharge by frustration in the following circumstances.

- If alternative mode of performance still possible
  - *Tsakiroglou & Co v Noblee and Thorl GmbH 1962*

- If performance becomes more expensive
  - *Davis Contractors v Fareham UDC 1956*

- If one party accepts the risk that he will be unable to perform
  - *Budgett & Co v Binnington & Co 1891*

- If one party induces frustration by his own choice between alternatives
  - *Maritime National Fish v Ocean Trawlers 1935*

Effects

Common law provides that, on frustration, the contract is brought to immediate end. This can lead to a harsh result (contract is not void *ab initio* and the loss lies where it falls).

The doctrine was modified in 1942 so that a contract was held void *ab initio* if total failure of consideration.

* *Fibrosa v Fairbairn 1942*

Regulation is now by Law Reform (Frustrated Contracts) Act 1943.

* Any money already paid can be recovered (subject to rule on expenses)

* Any sums still due cease to be payable

* Party liable to repay money may set off expenses incurred up to the time of frustration

* If one party has obtained a valuable benefit, court may order payment for this

---

Exam focus. In May 1996 you were asked to describe the circumstances in which the doctrine of frustration provides an excuse for non-performance. You then had to apply the principles to a problem question.

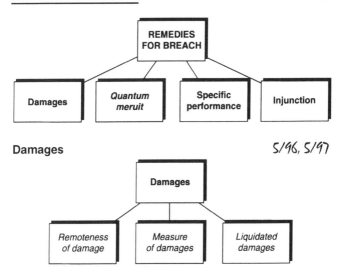

Damages 5/96, 5/97

Damages are a common law remedy designed to restore the injured party to the position he would have been in if the contract had been performed. Doctrine of restitution.

Remoteness of damage

How far down the sequence of cause and effect should the consequences of breach be traced? Apply the rule in *Hadley v Baxendale 1854*.

- Damages may be awarded in two circumstances
  - Where the loss arises naturally, according to the usual course of things
  - Where the loss arises in a manner which the parties may reasonably be supposed to have contemplated as the probable result of a breach of contract

- A loss outside the natural course of events will only be compensated if the exceptional circumstances causing it are within the defendant's knowledge, actual or constructive, when the contract was made
  - *Victoria Laundry (Windsor) v Newman Industries 1949*
  - *The Heron II 1969*

Measure of damages

As a general rule, plaintiff is put in position he would have achieved had the contract been performed. This is assessed by reference to actual loss suffered. The *available market rule* can often be applied.

- This rate measures the difference between contract price and market/current price at time set for delivery

- This is a *prima facie* rule which can be overridden
  - *Thompson Ltd v Robinson (Gunmakers) Ltd 1955*
  - *Charter v Sullivan 1957*

Non-financial losses can be compensated.

- *Jarvis v Swan Tours 1973*

But must be in proportion

- *Ruxley Electronics v Forsyth 1995*

Plaintiff must take reasonable steps to mitigate loss.

- *Payzu Ltd v Saunders 1919*

Liquidated damages

Parties may include a formula (liquidated damages) to determine the damages payable for breach. The formula will be enforced by courts if it is a 'genuine pre-estimate of loss', otherwise it is void as a penalty clause.

- *Dunlop Pneumatic Tyre Co v New Garage Co 1915*

- *Ford Motor Co (England) Ltd v Armstrong 1915*

Quantum meruit

This is a measure of the contractual value of the work which has been performed.

- Aims to restore plaintiff to position he would have been in if the contract had never been made

- Most likely to be sought if one party has performed his obligations and the other repudiates

Specific performance

This is an equitable remedy. The court may order defendant to perform his obligations under the contract. The order is made where court considers damages to be an inadequate remedy, for example, in respect of the sale of a particular piece of land.

It will not be made where contract requires supervision over period of time, as the Court cannot ensure full compliance.

Injunction

This is an equitable remedy. The court may order defendant to observe a negative restriction of a contract.

- *Warner Bros Pictures Inc v Nelson 1937*

Exam focus. Remedies were examined in November 96 for 12 marks. The question then tested damages in a problem for 6 marks. In May 1997 remoteness of damage and quantification of damages were tested.

Agency is no longer specifically examinable from May 1999, but still has relevance for companies and partnerships.

Directors and, to a lesser extent, the company secretary are agents of the company with actual authority to make contracts.

Duties of directors as agents

The director as agent has a fiduciary duty. Must not abuse the confidence of another (ie the company and shareholders) for whom he is acting.

- Duty of performance

- Duty of obedience

- Duty of skill. He must maintain standard of skill and care to be expected of a person in his profession

- Duty of personal performance. He may not delegate, unless this is necessary in the ordinary course of business

- Duty of accountability

- Duty not to put himself in situation of conflict of interest
  - *Armstrong v Jackson 1917*

- Duty of confidentiality

- Duty to hand over any benefit, unless agreed by principal
  - *Boston Deep Sea Fishing and Ice Co v Ansell 1888*

Every partner is an agent of the firm and of his other partners

- His acts in carrying on the firm's business in the usual way bind the firm and his partners

- The partner must have authority and the person he deals with must know he has authority

- A partner may be bound if his transaction is of the usual/expected kind, and the other party is unaware of any actual limits to his authority

Elements of negligence

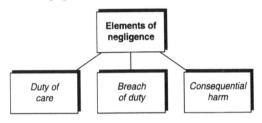

To succeed in an action for negligence, plaintiff must prove

- The defendant owed him a duty of care
- That duty was breached by the defendant
- As a result the plaintiff suffered injury or damage

Duty of care

Concept stems from *Donoghue v Stevenson 1932*. Lords ruled that a person might owe a duty of care to another with whom he had no contractual relationship at all. The doctrine has been much refined in the intervening period and current law is set out in a number of recent cases.

- *Murphy v Brentwood DC 1990*
- *Caparo Industries plc v Dickman and Others 1990*

The duty is based on the need for a sufficient relationship of proximity between the parties. Courts will also consider whether there are reasons of public policy for negating or reducing class of persons to whom a duty is owed.

In particular, courts are reluctant to hold that a duty of care exists in cases of economic loss and nervous shock.

- Economic loss is financial loss which is not consequential upon physical injury to persons or property
  - Loss of profits not recoverable
    - *Muirhead v Industrial Tank Specialists 1986*
  - Exceptionally, if special relationship 'akin to contract' claim may succeed
    - *Junior Books v Veitchi Co Ltd 1983*
  - Similarly, claim may succeed where plaintiff specifically in defendant's direct contemplation
    - *Ross v Caunters 1980*

- As regards nervous shock, it was originally thought necessary for plaintiff to fear injury to self or near relative and for plaintiff actually to witness act itself
  - Plaintiff may witness immediate aftermath
    - *McLoughlin v O'Brien 1982*
  - May be damage to property
    - *Attia v British Gas plc 1987*
  - Distinction between those present at event and those who witness it viewing live television
    - *Alcock v Chief Constable of South Yorkshire Police 1991*

No duty of care is owed by fire authorities to individual property owners

- *Nelson Holdings v British Gas 1997*

Breach of duty

Standard of reasonable care requires that defendant should have done what a reasonable man 'guided upon those considerations which ordinarily regulate the conduct of human affairs' would do.

- Standard of a reasonable man varies
  - o If faced with emergency, may take risks, for example, a fireman speeding to fire
  - o Test is based on knowledge at time, not hindsight
    - – *Roe v Minister of Health 1954*
  - o Standard higher if known that plaintiff unusually vulnerable ('thin skull')
    - – *Paris v Stepney Borough Council 1951*

- The plaintiff may argue that the facts speak for themselves (*res ipsa loquitur*)
  - o 'Thing' under control of defendant
  - o Accident would not have happened if proper care had been exercised
    - – *Scott v London & St Katharine Docks Co 1865*

Consequential harm

The plaintiff must show that, as a result of the breach of duty, he has suffered some damage.

- The damage must be *caused* to a substantial extent by the defendant's conduct; this is a question of fact

- The damage must not be too *remote* from the breach; this is a question of law

Causation and remoteness are different parts of the same series of events. Once causation has been shown, the defendant may seek to show that there is not a sufficiently close connection between his action and the damage caused, ie that the loss is too remote.

- Test of reasonable foreseeability: what would a reasonable man have foreseen as the consequences of the tort

- o The Wagon Mound 1961
- o The test is an objective one
- o The test is wider (more generous to the plaintiff) than the test for remoteness of damage under contract law, which states that the loss must be foreseeable as the probable result of the breach
  - – *Hughes v Lord Advocate 1963*
  - – *Doughty v Turner Manufacturing Co 1964*
- Novus actus interveniens: chain of events may be broken by an intervening event
  - o May be act of the plaintiff
  - o May be a third party over whom the defendant had no control

Specific applications   *11/95, 11/96, 11/97*

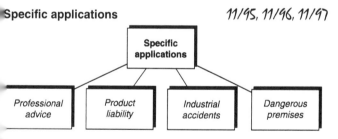

Professional advice

There is a duty of care not to cause economic loss by negligent misstatement. Rule of liability is slightly different. The test is based on a *special relationship* between the parties.

The statement must be made in some professional or expert capacity which makes it likely that another person will rely on it.

- *Chaudry v Prabhakar 1989*

The maker of statement must foresee that it is likely to be relied upon by another person.

- *Hedley Byrne v Heller and Partners 1964*

The tightening of the liability test as exemplified by *Murphy Brentwood DC 1990* is also apparent in respect of professiona advice. In *Caparo Industries plc v Dickman and Others 1990*, th House of Lords acknowledged that liability for negligent aud can exist, but stated requirement for following factors.

- Advice required for purpose made known to adviser whe advice given

- Adviser knows advice will be communicated to recipient i order to be used for this purpose

- Adviser knows advice likely to be relied on withou independent enquiry

- Advice is acted on to detriment of recipient

In the *Caparo* case, there was insufficient proximity betwee auditors and public at large (including shareholders).

Caparo upheld in *McNaughton (James) Papers Group Ltd Hicks Anderson and Co 1991*. Court of Appeal held tha although accountants were aware of possible takeover, the were unaware that accounts would be relied on without furthe advice.

A verbal assurance that an auditor 'stands by' the audit ca create proximity and the auditors can be found liable.

- *ADT v Binder Hamlyn 1995*

Exam focus. Professional negligence was examined in November 1996 in a question based around the Binder Hamlyn case. It also came up in November 1997, so it is clearly a 'hot topic'.

Product liability 5/98

Three approaches available to consumer seeking to claim against manufacturer for damage due to defective goods.

- *Contractual claim* against vendor, perhaps on basis of statutory implied terms, could form one of a chain of actions

- *Claim in tort*, under which fault must be proven

- Claim under Consumer Protection Act 1987

> *Exam focus.* This area was examined in May 1998. The examiner was disappointed that candidates often made reference to only one of the above three approaches.

Act imposes strict civil liability for defective goods. There is no need to prove negligence or show a contractual relationship. The following must be shown.

- The product contained defect
- The plaintiff suffered damage
- The defect caused the damage
- The defendant was producer, 'own-brander' or importer

A defect exists if the product is not as safe as it is reasonable to expect, taking into account all circumstances, including advertising, time of supply, anticipated normal use and provision of instructions.

Consumers and other users can claim for death, personal injury or damage to property (not to product itself).

Within 3 years of fault becoming apparent

Within 10 years of original supply

- Any claim for damage to property must
  - Not be for business property
  - Be for damage over £275

Defences are available.

- Defect attributable to compliance with enactment

- Product was not supplied to another

- Supply was otherwise than in the course of a business

- Defect did not exist at time of supply

- State of scientific and technical knowledge was such th
  manufacturer could not detect fault

- Defect attributable to design of subsequent product in
  which product incorporated

Industrial accidents

An employer may be liable in tort to his employee if employ
injured.

- Employer's failure to take reasonable care in providing
  - Safe premises and plant
  - Safe system of work
  - Competent fellow employees

- Employer's breach of a statutory duty
  - Example: Factories Act 1961

Dangerous premises　　　　　　　　　　　　　　　　　　*11/9*

An occupier has a duty to lawful visitors under Occupie
Liability Act 1957 and to trespassers under Occupiers' Liabi
Act 1984.

Lawful visitors

- o Occupier is person in control of the premises
    - *Wheat v Lacon & Co Ltd 1966*
- o Premises include land and buildings and fixed and moveable structures, for example, mechanical digger, scaffolding and a lift
- o Visitors are persons lawfully on the premises, for example, customer in shop, technician doing a repair
- o Occupier must ensure visitor is reasonably safe in using premises for permitted purpose
    - Higher standard of care for children
    - Person doing his job can be expected to be aware of special risks arising from this
    - No liability for faulty works of an independent contractor, provided ensured contractor competent

Trespassers: before 1984, there was a duty to act with common sense and humanity

- o *British Railways Board v Herrington 1972*
- o Occupier owes duty under Act if
    - Aware of danger or has reasonable grounds to believe it exists
    - Knows or should know that someone may come into vicinity of danger
    - Should reasonably be expected to offer other person protection against the risk
- o Occupier only liable for injury to person, not for loss or damage to property
- o Duty may be discharged by taking reasonable steps to give warning of the danger

Exam focus. In a question on product liability, such as the one which appeared in November 1995, it may be important to consider the position in contract and tort as well as under CPA 1987.

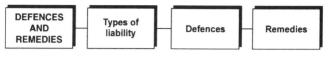

Types of liability   5/95

Under the principles of *strict liability*, the defendant may be liable even if he took reasonable care. Proof of the wrongful act is enough.

The best example is given by the rule in *Rylands v Fletcher 1868*. Where person keeps on land anything likely to do mischief if it escapes, he must keep it in at his peril and if he fails to do so he is liable for all damage naturally accruing from the escape.

- Relates to non-natural use of land, for example water, chemicals, animals

- Polluters may be strictly liable in nuisance, rendering *Rylands v Fletcher* unnecessary

  o *Cambridge Water Co v Eastern Counties Leather plc 1994*

A person may also have a civil remedy by way of an action in tort for a *breach of statutory duty*.

- Plaintiff must show the following

  o Statute was intended to give a civil remedy for breach

  o Defendant in breach

  o As a consequence plaintiff suffered harm which was not too remote

- Under the Factories Act 1961 there is an absolute duty to fence securely all prime movers

Under the principles of *vicarious liability*, for employer to be liable for tort of an employee, it is necessary that

- There is a relationship between them of employer and employee (refer **Chapter 11**)

- The employee's tort was committed in the course of his employment

For the tort to have been committed in the course of employment, the employee must have been doing the work for which he was employed.

- Employer liable even if employee disobeys orders as to how he shall do his work
  - *Limpus v London General Omnibus Co 1862*
    - Bus driver breaking rules
  - *Beard v London General Omnibus Co 1900*
    - Conductor driving bus

- Employer liable if employee, while engaged on duties, does something for own convenience
  - *Century Insurance v Northern Ireland Road Transport Board 1942*
    - Explosion from lighted match
  - *Warren v Henleys 1948*
    - Quarrel with customer

- If employer allows employee to use employer's vehicle for own affairs, employer not liable for any accident
  - *Twine v Bean's Express 1946*
    - Passenger given lift against rules
  - *Rose v Plenty 1976*
    - Boy helping with deliveries

Defences

A defence need only be argued once the basic requirements of the tort have been established by the plaintiff.

- *Volenti non fit injuria* (consent)
  - Express or implied consent to the risk of injury
    - *ICI v Shatwell 1965*
  - Mere knowledge does not imply consent
    - *Smith v Baker & Sons 1891*
  - In rescue cases, there is no consent where risk taken to safeguard others
    - *Haynes v Harwood & Son 1935*
    - *Cutler v United Dairies 1933*

- Accident, that is where event could not have been foreseen, nor avoided by any reasonable care
  - *Stanley v Powell 1891*

- Act of God. This is very rare

- Act of State, where loss or damage caused in course of duties for the State
  - *Buron v Denman 1848*

- Necessity, where the act is reasonable in order to prevent greater evil

- Mistake, where the defendant has acted reasonably and made mistake
  - Example: false imprisonment

- Self defence, involving reasonable force (retaliation is never reasonable)

Where there is contributory negligence by the plaintiff, his claim will be proportionately reduced.

Remedies

The main remedy is damages, representing compensation to the plaintiff for his financial loss.

- Compensatory damages
  - Put plaintiff in position he would have been in if tort had not been committed
  - Ordinary damages depend on court's view of nature of plaintiff's injury. Examples:
    - Loss of amenity
    - Pain and suffering
    - Loss of expectation of life
  - Special damages can be positively proven. Examples:
    - Damage to clothing
    - Cost of car repairs

- Exemplary damages include an element of punishment, for example, where newspaper publishes defamatory statement in expectation that profits will outweigh damages

- Nominal damages are awarded where no actual loss is suffered. For example: £1 in recognition of fact that plaintiff suffered a wrong

An injunction is an equitable remedy. It is an order of the court requiring individual to act in a certain way or refrain from so doing.

Exam focus. Remember that aspects of vicarious liability are just as likely to be examined in the context of an employment law question as here.

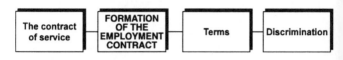

The contract of service   *11/96*

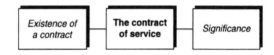

Existence of a contract

Important to determine whether a person is an employee under a contract of service or an independent contractor.

- Factors considered by courts
    - Reality of the situation
        - *Ferguson v John Dawson & Partners 1976*
    - Agreement between parties, provided it reflects underlying situation
        - *Massey v Crown Life Assurance 1978*
- Tests applied
    - Control test: does employer control way in which duties performed?
        - *Mersey Docks & Harbour Board v Coggins & Griffiths (Liverpool) 1947*
    - Integration test: employer may be unable to control skilled 'employee'. Is the employee integrated into employer's organisation?
        - *Cassidy v Ministry of Health 1951*

- o Economic reality test: is the employee working on his own account?

  - *Ready Mixed Concrete (South East) v Minister of Pensions and National Insurance 1968*

Significance

Reasons why the distinction is important.

- Social security contributions
- Income tax treatment
- Entitlement to employment protection
- Liability for tortious acts
- Implied terms in the contract
- Registration for VAT
- Rights in event of bankruptcy
- Health and safety

> *Exam focus.* This was examined in both essay and problem form in November 1996. The distinction can be examined either in the context of employment law or in the area of negligence (liability of an employer for employee's acts).

Terms   11/95, 11/97

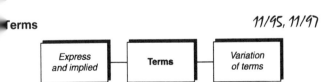

Express and implied

Express terms are those expressly agreed between the parties. A written statement of prescribed particulars must be given to employee within two months of beginning of employment.

- If written contract given covering prescribed points, no need for separate written particulars

- If change made to terms in written particulars, employer must within one month provide written statement of the change

- If employer fails to comply, employee may apply to industrial tribunal for declaration of what the terms should be

There are also *implied* duties on both sides.

- Employer's duties are as follows
    o Pay a reasonable remuneration
    o Provide itemised payslips
    o Indemnity for re-imbursement of expenses properly incurred
    o Provision of work
    o References: no duty but must take reasonable care when a reference is provided
    o Health and safety: implied common law duty to provide safe premises and plant, safe system of work and competent fellow employees

- Employee's duties are as follows
    o Fundamental duty of faithful service

        – *Hivac Ltd v Park Royal Scientific Instruments Ltd 1946*

    o Reasonable competence to do the job
    o Obedience to employer's instructions, unless unlawful personal danger

        – *Ottoman Bank Ltd v Chakarian 1930*

- *Bouzourou v Ottoman Bank Ltd 1930*
  - Duty to account
    - *Boston Deep Sea Fishing and Ice Co v Ansell 1888*
  - Reasonable care and skill
  - Personal service

- Collective implied terms are as follows
  - Agreements between unions and employer are not usually legally binding
  - Areas such as tasks and working conditions

- Statutory implied terms are as follows
  - Wages (wages councils now abolished)
  - Maternity leave
    - Paid time off for ante-natal care
    - Protection against dismissal for reasons connected with pregnancy
    - Up to 40 weeks' maternity leave
    - Up to 18 weeks' SMP
    - Right to return to old job
  - Time off work
    - With pay: union official carrying out duties; employees given notice of dismissal for redundancy
    - Without pay: union members for union activities; employees carrying out public duties, eg magistrates
  - Health and safety
    - Factories Act 1961
    - Health and Safety at Work Act 1974

Variation of terms

A change in contract terms can only be made with the consent of both parties to the contract.

- *No change* to contract: may be possible to vary contract terms without varying contract, for example, where express term in contract gives rights of variation
  - Term may be implied to give contract business efficacy, for example, a sales rep may be allocated to new area to meet changing market conditions
  - Term may be implied by custom, for example a steel erector may be required to change sites

- *A change* to the contract requires consent. Employer might seek to issue ultimatum
  - Employee can then consent
  - Employee can continue working making clear that he does not accept variation
  - Employee can claim constructive dismissal

- Signing *a new contract* opens employer to potential claim for unfair dismissal

> *Exam focus.* This material on variation of terms is very important, as it combines legal rules with very practical issues. This makes it ideal for a 'hypothetical but realistic' scenario.

Discrimination   *11/95*

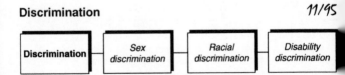

Sex discrimination

Sex Discrimination Act 1975 prohibits discrimination on grounds of gender against any employee, male or female, in the recruitment, promotion, training, benefits or dismissal of employees. Two kinds of discrimination are prohibited.

- Direct discrimination, where the employer or prospective employer treats an employee or job applicant less favourably than another on grounds of sex

- Indirect discrimination
  - *Price v Civil Service Commission 1978*

There are exceptions. It is permissible to discriminate if there is a genuine occupational qualification.

- Decency/privacy

- Customs overseas

Under the Equal Pay Act 1970, contractual employment terms given to a man or woman should be at least as favourable as those given to an employee of the opposite sex.

Racial discrimination

Discrimination on grounds of race is prohibited by Race Relations Act 1976. Similar provisions to SDA 1975.

Disability discrimination

  - The Disability Discrimination Act 1995 gives disabled people similar rights to those enjoyed with regard to race and sex.

Exam focus. Discrimination at work is highly topical. Make sure you are up to date with developments. This examiner likes candidates who can demonstrate 'modern' knowledge.

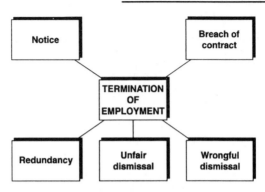

Notice

A contract may be terminated by notice. Period of notice must not be less than statutory minimum.

- Employee continuously employed for one month or more but less than two years: not less than one week's notice

- Employee continuously employed for two years or more but less than twelve years: not less than one week's notice for each year

- Employee continuously employed for twelve years or more: not less than twelve weeks' notice

- If employee gives notice, minimum period is one week

Breach of contract   *11/98*

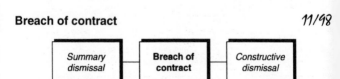

Summary dismissal

The employee is dismissed without notice. The employer is justified if employee has committed serious breach of contract. This will depend on circumstances.

- *Pepper v Webb 1969*
- *Wilson v Racher 1974*

Constructive dismissal

The employer repudiates some essential term of the contract, for example by unilateral imposition of change in employee's duties. The employee resigns and the employer is then liable for breach.

- Employee must show the following
  - Employer's breach
  - Employee left because of the breach
  - No affirmation of contract by employee

Wrongful dismissal   5/98

Action derived from common law rights in contract. Brought in county court or High Court. (Note that industrial tribunal may now also hear contractual claims under £25,000.)

- Examples include the following
  - Where there has been a summary dismissal
  - Where employer dismisses with insufficient notice
- Employer will seek to show justification of dismissal
  - Wilful disobedience of lawful order, if wilful and serious defiance of authority
  - Misconduct, usually in connection with the business
  - Incompetence

Remedies are limited to a claim for damages based on loss of earnings. May be more attractive than claim for relatively low amounts available as compensation for unfair dismissal.

The court will not grant order for specific performance in a contract for personal services.

Unfair dismissal   *5/98, 11/98*

This concept was created by employment protection legislation. Increased range of remedies available. Employee must show three things.

- Qualifying employee (some categories excluded)
    - Under normal retiring age
    - Relevant period of continuous employment
- Dismissal
    - Actual dismissal, usually clear from words used
    - Constructive dismissal
    - Expiry of a fixed-term contract without renewal
- Unfairly dismissed

Employer may be able to justify dismissal as fair. To succeed in this, must also demonstrate that acted reasonably, applying correct procedures and taking all circumstances into consideration.

- Potentially fair reasons are as follows
    - Capability or qualifications of employee
        - *Lewis Shops Group Ltd v Wiggins 1973*
    - Misconduct
    - Redundancy
    - Legal prohibition, for example a solicitor is struck off

- o Some other substantial reason, for example an employee is married to a competitor

- Automatically unfair reasons

  - o Pregnancy: this amounts to gender discrimination contrary to EC directive 76/207

    - – *Webb v Emo Air Cargo (UK) Ltd 1994*

  - o Trade union membership/activities

  - o Refusal to join trade union

  - o Staff may not be disadvantaged by reason of their performance of designated health and safety functions under the Management of Health and Safety at Work Regulations 1994

Remedies

Employee must present complaint to industrial tribunal within three months of termination. Three remedies are available.

- Re-instatement: return to same job with no break of continuity

- Re-engagement: new employment with same employer on terms specified in the order. This is rare

- Compensation, in three stages

  - o Basic award
  - o Compensatory award
  - o Punitive additional award

Exam focus. Unfair dismissal continues to be an increasingly important topic in 'real life' employment law. Make sure that you can discuss it from the point of view of employer *and* employee.

Redundancy

Dismissal is treated as redundancy in two circumstances.

- The employer has ceased, or intends to cease, to carry on business in which employee employed

- The requirements for employees to do that type of work have ceased or diminished. The test is whether the job still exists
    o *North Riding Garages v Butterwick 1967*

The employer may offer redundant employee alternative employment for future.

- The employee loses redundancy pay if unreasonably refuses

- There must be alternative employment in same capacity, location terms, conditions as previously

Employers must generally inform and consult an employee representative.

    o The remedy is redundancy pay, calculated on a statutory scale.

Exam focus. Link your studies on redundancy and unfair dismissal to the material on remedies, as they are likely to be examined together.

Regulations   5/96

Various pieces of legislation govern health and safety.

* Under s 2 Health and Safety at Work Act 1974, it is the duty of every employer, as far as is practicable, to ensure the health, safety and welfare of all his employees

* Factories Act 1961 applies to places where manufacturing or processing work is done

* Offices, Shops and Railway Premises Act 1973 also applies to certain premises

Additionally, many new regulations implementing EC Directives.

* Management of Health and Safety at Work Regulations 1992

* Workplace (Health, Safety and Welfare) Regulations 1992

* Health and Safety (Display Screen Equipment) Regulations 1992

Exam focus. Do not neglect this topic, particularly in the context of employment protection. The May 96 paper contained a question on health and safety law with particular reference to the employer's responsibilities in respect of injuries to employees.

Enforcement

HSC oversees the working of the system.
HSE appoints and controls inspectors.

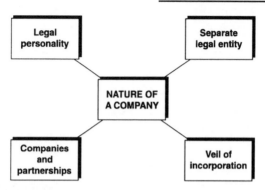

Legal personality

A person possesses legal rights and is subject to legal obligations. An individual human being is a natural person; the law also recognises artificial persons in the form of corporations.

- Corporations sole
    - Official positions
    - Example: the Public Trustee

- Chartered corporations (eg CIMA)

- Statutory corporations
    - Formed by Act of Parliament
    - Used in C19 to form railway and canal companies

- Registered companies, registered under CA 1985

Separate legal entity   *5/96, 11/96, 11/97*

Consequence of registration is that company becomes a legal person distinct from its owners (members).

- *Salomon v Salomon & Co Ltd 1897*

- Principal advantage is limited liability of members (*not* company)

- Characteristics of a company
  - Transferable shares
  - Perpetual succession
  - Assets, rights and liabilities belong to company, not to members
    - *Macaura v Northern Assurance Co Ltd 1925*
  - Capital retained
  - Supervision under CA 1985
  - Management entrusted to directors
  - Written constitution
  - Liable in tort and crime
    - *R v Kite, Stoddart and OLL Ltd 1994*
    - *Mousell Bros v London & North Western Railway 1917*

Veil of incorporation   *11/97*

The veil of incorporation is a term used to denote the distinction between a company and its members. Exceptions are made in certain circumstances either to identify the company with certain persons (eg directors or members) or to treat a group of companies as a single entity.

- Lifting the veil by statute to enforce the law
  - Liability of a sole member for a company's debts
    - s 24 CA 1985
    - Public companies only
  - Fraudulent trading
    - Where it appears that business carried on with intent to defraud creditors
    - Directors may be held personally responsible for debts and other liabilities
    - s 213 Insolvency Act 1986
  - Trading without trading certificate under s117 CA 1985
  - Re-use of name of insolvent company by its directors
    - Directors and company liable
    - s 216 Insolvency Act 1986
  - Use of company name in incorrect form (minor typing errors will not mean veil lifted)
    - s 349 CA 1985
    - *Penrose v Martyr 1858*
    - *Jenice Ltd v Dan 1993* (minor typing errors)
- Identification of a company and its members
  - Evasion of obligations imposed by law
    - *Gilford Motor Co Ltd v Horne 1933*
    - *Jones v Lipman 1962*
  - Used to conceal nationality
    - *Daimler Co Ltd v Continental Tyre and Rubber Co Ltd 1916*
    - *Re FG Films Ltd 1953*
  - Evasion of liabilities

- – *Creasey v Breachwood Motors Ltd 1992*
  - o Evasion of taxation
    - – *Unit Construction Co Ltd v Bullock 1960*
  - o Quasi-partnership
    - – *Ebrahimi v Westbourne Galleries Ltd 1973*

- Groups of companies (only if one agent/trustee of other, or together they carry on a single business)
  - o *Firestone Tyre & Rubber Co Ltd v Lewellin 1957*
  - o *DHN Food Distributors Ltd v Tower Hamlets LBC 1976*
  - o *Adams v Cape Industries plc 1990*: identification of group members as single entity only applies in limited circumstances.

- Holding company giving a 'comfort letter' on subsidiary's debts not liable for those debts
  - o *Kleinwort v Malaysian Mining Corporation 1989*

Exam focus. The November 1996 paper asked for a discussion of the continuing applicability of the *Salomon* judgement. Question 6 in November 1997 asked about lifting the veil of incorporation.

Companies and partnerships

Characteristics

Partnership is the relation which subsists between persons carrying on a business in common with a view of profit. Partners are liable without limit for the debts of the partnership

- Statutory maximum of 20 partners in commercial, not professional, partnerships

- Terms implied by Partnership Act 1890 unless varied or excluded by partnership agreement

Differences between partnerships and companies

Company	Partnership
Separate entity	No separate entity
Members' liability limited	Partners' liability usually unlimited
Perpetual succession - no cessation by change of membership	A change of partners is termination of the old firm and beginning of new one
Company (not members) own assets	Partners jointly own partnership property
A company must have one or more directors. Members do not necessarily manage	Partners are entitled to participate in management and are agents of the firm
A company always has a written constitution	A partnership may exist without any written partnership agreement
Usually, a company must deliver annual accounts, annual returns and other notices to Registrar of Companies	A partnership must disclose the names of the partners. But no one except a partner has any right to inspect accounts

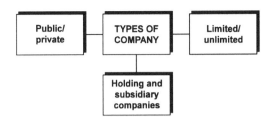

Public/private

A private company is a limited company with at least one member. Companies are private unless specifically registered as public.

- Public company must satisfy the following

  - Registration as public company
  - At least two members
  - Statement in memorandum that public company

- Main differences

  - Minimum share capital of public company is £50,000

  - Public company name ends in 'public limited company' or 'plc'

  - Rules on issue of capital and payment for shares

  - Rules on dividends

  - Public company must have at least two directors and at least two members

  - Rules on preparation and filing of accounts

  - Rules on commencement of business

- A public company may be *listed* on the Stock Exchange

Limited/unlimited

Liability is usually limited by shares. May be limited instead by guarantee, whereby memorandum states amount each member will contribute in the event of a liquidation.

- Appropriate for non-commercial undertaking

- Examples: charity or trade association

A company may be formed with unlimited liability. The memorandum makes no reference to liability of members. Members are required to contribute as much as is necessary to enable company to pay its debts in the event of a liquidation.

Advantages

- No need to file report and accounts

- Convenient vehicle to hold assets, eg on behalf of a partnership

Holding and subsidiary companies

A company is the subsidiary (S) of another company, its holding company (H) if:

- H holds majority of voting rights in S

- H is a member of S and has the right by voting control to remove/appoint majority of S's board of directors

- H is a member of S and controls a majority of the voting rights by agreement with other members/shareholders

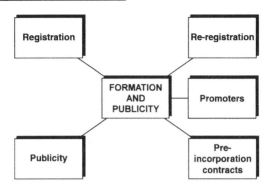

Registration *5/95, 11/95*

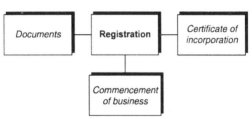

Documents

Certain documents must be sent to the Registrar of Companies.

- Memorandum signed by the subscribers to the memorandum

- Articles or a statement of intention to adopt Table A

- Form 10 setting out details of:
  - Registered office
  - Director(s) and secretary

- Form 12 - a statutory declaration that all the requirements for registration have been met

- A fee of £20

Exam focus. However 'selective' your revision, do not leave out the topic of documents to be sent to the Registrar. It may come up as part of a larger question.

Certificate of incorporation

If everything is in order the Registrar will issue a certificate of incorporation (and publish notice of it in the *London Gazette*). The company's life dates from the date on the certificate of incorporation.

- *Jubilee Cotton Mills Ltd v Lewis 1924*

Commencement of business

- A private company can start business immediately.

- A public company must convince the Registrar it has sufficient monies and must provide three extra details
  - Share capital
  - Preliminary expenses
  - Amount due or paid to promoters

- If everything is in order the Registrar will issue a trading certificate under s 117 and publish notice of it in the *Gazette*.

- If a public company starts trading without satisfying s 117 there are four consequences.
  - The company is primarily liable

- o If the company does not meet its liabilities within 21 days of demand being made, the directors have personal liability
- o The company and its officers are liable to a fine
- o If a s 117 certificate is not obtained within one year of incorporation it is grounds for winding up under s 122 (1)(b) Insolvency Act 1986

Re-registration

Public to private: s 53

This requires the following.

- A special resolution
- Alteration of the memorandum and articles
- Application in a prescribed form

The Registrar issues a new certificate of incorporation and Gazettes it.

Minority protection is available.

Private to public: s 43

The company must do the following.

- Pass a special resolution
- Alter the memorandum and articles
- Satisfy share capital/net assets requirements

Promoters

A promoter is anyone who facilitates the formation of a company.

Duties

- A common law duty to exercise reasonable skill and care.

- Equitable fiduciary duties:
  - To disclose to the company any interest which the promoter has in a transaction entered into by the company
  - Not to make any profits out of the promotion of the company without the company's consent

Disclosure of profits

- *Either* to an independent board of directors: *Erlanger v New Sombrero Phosphates Co 1878*. This can be impractical as the first directors are liable to be friends, relatives and business associates

- *Or* to the existing and potential members: *Gluckstein v Barnes 1900*

Remuneration of promoters

Promoters may have a problem being paid as they have no contract with the company. At the time of doing their work the latter does not exist.

Pre-incorporation contracts

A registered company has no existence until its certificate of incorporation has been issued. Persons cannot contract on behalf of something which does not exist.

S 36 says that (unless there is an exclusion clause) a person who signs a pre-incorporation contract is personally liable. It does not matter in whose name the document is signed.

- *Phonogram v Lane 1981*

Ratification by the company

- Companies cannot ratify pre-incorporation contracts
  - *Natal Land and Colonisation Co v Pauline Colliery (and Development) Syndicate 1904*

- A new contract between the third party and the company can be produced ('novation')

- The existence of a new contract may be implied (eg by re-negotiation of payment terms)
  - *Howard v Patent Ivory Manufacturing Co 1888*

- Purchase of an off the shelf company can alleviate problem as company will have been incorporated when the contract was made

Publicity

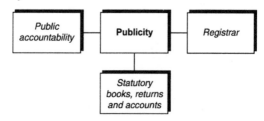

Public accountability

Public accountability is the price which a company pays for limited liability. It takes the following forms.

● File at Companies Registry

● Registers and other documents

● *London Gazette*

● Company's letterheads and other forms, which must give place of registration, registration number

Note that a company is also accountable to its *members* in ways covered elsewhere.

Registrar

The Registrar of Companies is head of a division of the DTI. He keeps the company's file and must give notice of various matters (covered elsewhere) in the *London Gazette*.

Statutory books, returns and accounts

Registers

Those items marked * must be kept at the registered office.

- Register of members

- Register of directors and secretaries*

- Register of directors' interests in shares/debentures

- Register of charges*

- Minutes of company general meetings*

- Minutes of directors' and managers' meetings

- Register of written resolutions*

- For public companies - register of substantial interests (≥ 3%) in shares.

Exam focus. A possible 'part (a)' of a question : 'What are the registers which a limited company must keep?'

Returns

- Annual return, which is a summary of essential information
  o Address of registered office
  o Type of company and its business
  o Number of issued shares
  o Names and addresses of directors and secretary; directors' date of birth, nationality, other directorships held
  o Whether dispensed with laying of accounts before general meeting or holding AGM (private companies only)
  o Members (full list need only be given once every three years; otherwise just changes / share transfers)

- Change in directors or secretaries or their particulars

- Return of allotments

Annual accounts

The directors must, in respect of each accounting reference period of the company:

- Prepare balance sheet and profit and loss account
- Lay accounts before company in general meeting
- Deliver copy of accounts to registrar

The form and content of the accounts is covered in your studies for Paper 5 *Financial Accounting*

Accounting records

Proper accounting records must be kept to fulfil the above obligations. They must make it possible to:

- Determine with reasonable accuracy the company's financial position
- Ascertain that P&L and B/S in accordance with the Act

Directors may be disqualified if proper accounting records are not kept.

- *Re Firedart Ltd, Official Receiver v Fairall 1994.*

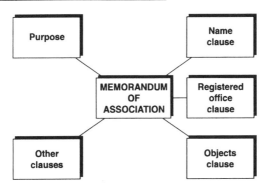

Purpose

11/98

The memorandum defines the company's relationships with third parties. The six principal clauses are as follows.

- Name
- Registered office
- Objects
- Limited liability
- Share capital
- Association

> *Exam focus.* Question 8 (a) in November 1998 asked about the legal effect of writing conditions into the Memorandum of Association.

Name clause

This obviously sets out the company's name.

Refusal to register

By s 26 the Registrar may refuse to register a name which has any of the following features

- Offensive (in the opinion of the Registrar)

- Constitutes an offence (prohibited by statute)

- The same as an existing corporation (although a person can use his/her own name)

- Where the words require permission and this has not been provided. There are two types of such words

  o Those which imply a connection with the government or civil service

  o Those mentioned in the list in the *Business Names Act 1985* and *The Business Names Regulations 1981*

- Omits plc/limited

Passing off

There is a tort (called passing off) where a person carries on a business under a name that would mislead the public into believing the business is conducted by another person. The most common method is to trade under a similar name.

The injured party must prove that there is a genuine possibility of confusion (operate in similar business).

- *Ewing v Buttercup Margarine Co Ltd 1917*

Remedies are an injunction to prevent further violation and damages

The court tends to allow the use of a person's name who is directly involved with the company or words in common usage.

Changes of name

The name clause can be changed by special resolution. The Secretary of State can order a company to change its name:

- Within 12 months if the company has been inadvertently issued with a name similar to that of an existing company (s 28(2))

- Within five years if misleading information was supplied (s 28(3))

- At any time if the use of the name is likely to cause harm to the public (s 32)

A copy of the special resolution and the revised memorandum must be sent to the Registrar within 15 days. The Registrar alters the register, issues a new certificate of incorporation and advertises change in the *London Gazette*.

Publication of the name

The name must appear legibly and conspicuously in the following places.

- Outside the registered office and all places of business: s 348

- On the common seal (if the company has one): s 350

- On all business letters, notices and official publications

- On all bills of exchange, cheques, promissory notes, orders, receipts and invoices signed or issued on the company's behalf: s 349

Penalties

- A £300 fine for every officer wilfully authorising or permitting the breach.

- Personal liability for any person issuing any bill of exchange, promissory note, cheque or order for money/ goods without the correct company name.

  o *Penrose v Martyr 1858*

Limited liability

The name of a private company limited by shares must end with 'Limited' or 'Ltd': s 25.

The name of a public company must end with the words 'public limited company' or 'plc': s 25.

'Limited', 'Ltd', 'public limited company' or 'plc' must not appear anywhere except at the end of the name: s 26.

Registered office clause

Location

To be registered, the company's registered office must be in England and Wales or Scotland and the memorandum must say so.

No alteration of a company's memorandum in respect of the country of the registered office is permitted except by Act of Parliament.

Function

As the company's official address it is where legal documents, notices, and other communications may be served. Certain statutory books must be kept there.

Objects clause   *11/95, 5/96*

This sets out the objects (ie purpose) of company and defines the company's contractual capacity, also express powers (permissible transactions). It was designed to protect shareholders.

Prior to the Companies Acts 1985 and 1989, if a company entered into a contract which was outside its objects (*ultra vires)* that contract was void and unenforceable by either party to it.

Companies Act 1989

A company may in effect opt out of the *ultra vires* rule altogether by stating that the object of the company is to carry on business as 'a general commercial company': s 3A.

However, many companies still have traditional objects clauses, and therefore the rules as to *ultra vires* transactions are still relevant.

Remedies for an ultra vires transaction (s 35)

Remedies for shareholders

- Shareholders can restrain an *ultra vires* act by seeking an injunction. This can only be done *before* the act becomes binding

- They can sue directors for breach of duty

- They can ratify the *ultra vires* act by special resolution (NB they require a separate special resolution to absolve the directors from liability for breach of duty)

Remedies for third parties

- The doctrine of *ultra vires* has effectively been abolished

- *'The validity of an act done by a company shall not be called into question on the grounds of lack of capacity by reason of anything in the company's memorandum'*

- If third parties are acting in good faith, can assume board is able to bind company

---

Exam focus. Despite the fact that the law on *ultra vires* has been relaxed and simplified, the topic continues to be tested. You *must* remember that s 35 forms the basis of the current law.

Alteration of the objects clause

The objects can be altered by a special resolution: s 4.

A copy of the resolution must be sent to the Registrar within 15 days of its adoption.

Minority protection (s 5) is available.

Other clauses

Limited liability. This serves as a general notice to those dealing with the company. The liability of the members is limited to the amount *unpaid on their shares*.

Capital clause. This must state the amount of the share capital in £'s, the number of shares into which the share capital is divided and the nominal value of each share.

Association clause. This is a record and it cannot be altered. The subscribers simply sign to say that they are taking up a share in the company.

Points to note

- Plc's must state that they are plc's in the memorandum
- Any clause which is normally in the articles could be in the memorandum

Purpose and legal effect   *5/96, 11/98*

The articles are concerned with internal regulations of a company. Table A contains the specimen format and applies unless excluded expressly or by implication.

The articles constitute a contract between the following: s 14.

- Members and the company
  - *Hickman v Kent or Romney Marsh Sheepbreeders Association 1915,* compare *Beattie v Beattie 1938*

- The company and members
  - *Pender v Lushington 1877*

- The members *inter se*
  - *Cumbrian Newspapers Group Ltd 1986* case

  by series of mutual covenants
  - *Rayfield v Hands 1958*

The articles do not constitute a contract between the company and third parties.

- *Eley v Positive Life Co 1876*

However, they can be used to establish the terms of a contract existing elsewhere.

- *Re New British Iron Co, ex parte Beckwith 1898*

Alteration   *11/96*

The articles may be altered by a special resolution: s 9. The change cannot be prevented by declaring the articles/a clause to be unalterable. The basic test is whether the alteration is for the benefit of the company as a whole.

- *Greenhalgh v Arderne Cinemas 1950*

No outside contract will prevent a change but the company may be liable for breach of contract (eg breach of a director's service contract).

- *Southern Foundries v Shirlaw 1940*

Case law

- Most alterations are allowed by the court. An alteration will not be prevented simply because it inflicts hardship on some members but not on others
  - *Greenhalgh v Arderne Cinemas 1950*

- Alterations which give the company the power to expel members are viewed with considerable suspicion
  - *Dafen Tinplate Co v Llanelly Steel Co 1920*

- However, such alterations will be allowed if the proposed clause is carefully worded, eg where a member is:
  - competing with the company
    - *Sidebottom v Kershaw, Leese & Co Ltd 1920*
  - defrauding the company
    - *Shuttleworth v Cox Brothers Ltd 1927*

- Alterations can be prevented by 'weighted voting rights'
  - *Bushell v Faith 1970*

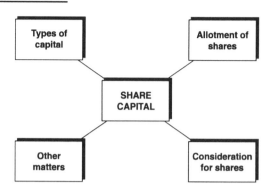

Types of capital

A share is a right to a specified amount of the share capital of a company, carrying with it certain rights and liabilities, while the company is a going concern and in its winding up.

It consists of a series of mutual covenants (*Borland's* case).

Share capital is a term used in a variety of senses.

- *Authorised share capital:* total amount of share capital which the company is authorised to issue

- *Issued share capital:* nominal value of shares which have been issued to members

- *Called up share capital:* aggregate amount of calls which a member is required to pay

- *Paid up share capital:* aggregate amount of money paid up on shares which have been issued

Note. The authorised share capital may be increased by resolution passed in general meeting. Table A (Art 32) requires only an ordinary resolution.

Loan capital is borrowed money obtained usually by the issue of debentures. It is a liability owed to creditors, whereas share capital represents the interest of the members of the company.

Allotment of shares   *11/95, 5/98*

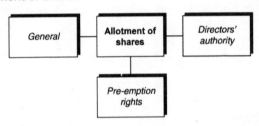

General

Share purchase or subscription is covered by contract law.

- An offer is made by the prospective shareholder
- Acceptance is when allotment is made by the company

Allotment is when a person obtains an unconditional right to be included in the company's register of members. A return of allotments (Form 88) must be lodged within one month of allotment.

A public company may not allot shares for subscription unless the offer is fully subscribed. Any moneys paid must be returned: s 84. If allotment has taken place, an allottee may avoid the contract within one month. This problem can be avoided by *underwriting*.

Directors' authority

The *authorised* share capital may be altered by ordinary resolution provided there is power in the articles: s 121.

Alteration of the *issued* share capital is more complicated, and is dealt with in s 80. This states that the directors of a company may not allot shares unless they are authorised to do so:

- By the articles; or
- By ordinary resolution (copy sent to Registrar)

The authority to allot may be particular/general; conditional/ unconditional.

- It must state:
  - The maximum number of shares which may be allotted
  - The date on which the authority expires

- It must not be for a period of more than five years from:
  - The date of incorporation (if authority was in the original articles)
  - The date of a resolution giving authority

- It can be extended beyond five years by private companies using an elective resolution, or it may be renewed for further periods of up to five years by any company subject to the same restrictions

- It may be revoked or varied at any time by the members in general meeting

Contravention of s 80

- Any director who contravenes or permits/authorises a contravention of s 80 will be liable to a fine

- This will not affect the validity of any allotment of shares: s 80(10)

Although the directors have the authority to allot shares they must remember their fiduciary duties to the company.

- They must act in the best interest of the company and issue shares for a proper purpose
  - *Howard Smith v Ampol Petroleum Ltd 1974*
- They must not allot to prevent a takeover
  - *Hogg v Cramphorn 1966*
- Unless sanctioned by a general meeting
  - *Bamford v Bamford 1969*

Pre-emption rights

Where *any* company (public or private) issues *equity shares wholly for cash*, it must first offer them to *existing equity shareholders* in proportion to the nominal value of their equity holding: s 89.

Holders of registered shares must receive notice in writing.

The offer must be open for at least 21 days.

No allotment may be made until:

- The offer period has expired; *or*
- Every offer made has been *accepted or refused:* s 90

Private companies will not be bound by s 89 if their memorandum or articles specifically exclude it.

If directors have either a general or specific authority to allot shares, then the company by special resolution may overrule or modify the rights.

This may require a written statement by the directors to be circularised with notice of the meeting.

Time limit on disapplication is 5 years

If securities are issued in breach of these rules, the members may recover loss from those in default - time limit two years.

Consideration for shares

The issue of shares at a discount is prohibited: s 100.

In general, shares in any company (public or private) may be paid up in *money* or *money's worth* (including goodwill and 'know-how'): s 99(1).

A private company may allot shares for inadequate consideration by acceptance of goods or services at an overvalue.

A public company may not allot shares unless at least 25% of their nominal value and the whole of any premium is paid up: s 101.

Shares in a public company may not be paid for by an undertaking to do work or to perform services: s 99(2).

Payment for shares by non-cash consideration

- A public company may not *allot* shares (whether as fully or partly paid) for a *non-cash* consideration (eg an asset such as a car or a painting), unless the company gets the asset within five years from the date of allotment: s 102

- A public company may not allot shares (whether as fully or partly paid) for a non-cash consideration unless:
  - The non-cash consideration has been independently valued; and

    o   A report on the valuation has been made to the company within the six month period prior to the allotment and to the allottee: s 103. The valuer must be the auditor or someone they consider to be suitably qualified

Liability for contravention of independent valuation rule

- Allottees are liable for any shortfall plus interest at 5%

- The court can give exemption (if it appears just and equitable to do so)

Share premium account: s 130

Where shares are issued at a premium whether for cash or otherwise, an amount equal to the premium must be transferred to a *share premium account*.

The account can be used for four purposes only.

- Writing off the preliminary expenses

- Writing off the expenses, commission or discount relating to any issue of shares or debentures

- Providing the premium payable on the redemption of shares or debentures

- Issuing fully paid bonus shares to existing members

Other matters

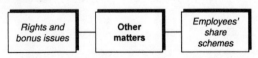

Rights and bonus issues

A *rights issue* is an allotment (or offer of allotment) of additional shares made to existing members. Rights not taken up can be sold on.

A *bonus issue* (capitalisation issue) is when a company applies its reserves to paying up unissued shares which are allotted to members.

Employees' share schemes

An employees' share scheme is one which facilitates the holding of shares in a company by or for *bona fide* employees or their spouses/widow(er)/minor children.

A company may allot ordinary shares for cash to such a scheme without first offering them to its general body of members.

Capital maintenance   *5/95, 11/95, 11/97, 11/98*

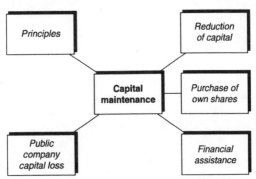

Principles

When members contribute capital to a company, it forms what is known as the *creditors' buffer*, funds on which creditors can draw if the company goes into liquidation. These funds cannot be 'distributed', ie given back to the members.

> *Exam focus.* Question 7(b) in November 1998 asked for a general explanation of the maintenance of capital principle.

Reduction of capital

A limited company may reduce its issued share capital provided that:

● It has powers to do so in its articles

- A special resolution is passed

- The court confirms the reduction under s 135

There are several methods of achieving such a reduction.

- Liability on partly paid shares may be extinguished by reducing the nominal value of the shares

- Where paid up share capital has been lost or is no longer represented by available assets, it may be cancelled

- Part of the paid up share capital may be paid off by reducing the nominal value of the shares

- Debenture stock may be issued to shareholders to achieve the effect of paying off parts of the paid up share capital

- All or part of the balance on an account comprising a statutory capital reserve (such as a share premium account) may be cancelled

The court then considers the reduction. If it is satisfied that the company will still be able to pay its debts, and that the result is fair in its effect on different classes of shareholders, it will give its approval.

Purchase of own shares

A company can purchase its own shares under the same rules as apply to redeemable shares (unless the result would be that only redeemable shares are left).

There are two methods of making such a purchase.

- A market purchase is a purchase under the normal arrangements of a recognised investment exchange

- An off-market purchase is any other purchase, usually by private treaty

A private limited company may redeem or purchase its shares out of capital by a 'permissible capital payment'.

- General authority must be given by the articles

- Capital can only be used to 'top up' distributable profits or the proceeds of a new issue, where such resources are insufficient. A capital redemption reserve may be required.

A complex procedure is prescribed to ensure that the company does not make itself insolvent.

- A statutory declaration from the directors is required (supported by a report from the auditors) stating that after the payment is made, the company will be able to pay its debts and continue its business for at least a year: s 173

- A special resolution must be passed. Any vendor of shares may not use the votes attached to shares which he is to sell to the company: s 173

- Application to the court may be made by any member who did not vote for the resolution (or any creditor) within five weeks to cancel the resolution: s 176

- A notice must be placed in the *Gazette* or an appropriate national newspaper, or every creditor must be informed: s 175

Exam focus. Question 6 in November 1997 asked about the various ways in which capital can be returned to members.

Financial assistance   5/96, 5/98

A public company may not give financial assistance to a third party to purchase shares in the company. A private company can do so under the following conditions.

- The financial assistance given must not reduce the net assets of the company, or, if it does, the assistance is to be provided from distributable profits

- A statutory declaration of solvency must be issued, under the same conditions as for a private company wishing to purchase its own shares out of capital

- A special resolution must be passed to approve the transaction

- Members holding at least 10% of the issued shares (or class of shares) have a right to apply to the court

This procedure is not available to any group of companies which includes a public company.

Two tests are applied to any suspect financial transactions by s 153.

- What was its purpose? It may not be objectionable if its primary purpose was not to provide financial assistance, and it is also an incidental part of some larger purpose of the company

- Did the directors act *bona fide* in the interests of the company (and not the third party)?

The following transactions are specifically exempted by s 153.

- Payment of a dividend out of profits

- Distribution of assets in a winding up

- Allotment of bonus shares

- Reduction of capital approved by the court

- Redemption or purchase of shares under the appropriate procedures

- Various transactions incidental to reconstruction, amalgamation and liquidation

> *Exam focus.* Do not confuse a company purchasing its own shares, and a company giving financial assistance for *someone else* to purchase its shares.

Public company capital loss

If the net assets of a public company drop to half or less of the amount of its called up share capital there must be an extraordinary general meeting:

- Called within 28 days; and

- Convened not less than 56 days after the relevant facts have come to light

Dividends   5/97

Table A articles provide that:

- Company in GM may declare dividends

- No dividend can exceed directors' recommended dividend

- Directors can declare interim dividends

Any provision of the articles for the declaration and payment of dividends is subject to the overriding rules of ss 263-281. Dividends may only be paid from distributable profits (s 263), which may be defined as:

- Accumulated realised profits less accumulated realised losses

- 'Accumulated' means that any losses of previous year must be included in reckoning the current distributable surplus

- 'Realised' generally means it is in accordance with generally accepted accounting principles at the time the accounts are prepared.

A public company may (in addition) only make a distribution if its net assets are, at the time, not less than the aggregate of its called up share capital and undistributable reserves (the 'full net worth test').

Undistributable reserves are defined by s 264 as follows.

- Share premium account

- Capital redemption reserve

- Any surplus of accumulated unrealised profits over accumulated unrealised losses

- Any further reserve which the company is prohibited from distributing by its memorandum or articles

The question of whether a company has profits from which to pay a dividend is determined by reference to its 'relevant accounts', which are generally its latest *audited* accounts.

Infringement of dividend rules

The directors may be liable to make good to the company the amount of an unlawful dividend in the following situations.

- Where they recommend or declare a dividend which they know is paid out of capital

- Where they recommend or declare a dividend out of capital without having previously prepared any accounts

- Where they have made a mistake of law or interpretation of the memorandum or articles (although they may obtain relief under s 727 for an act performed 'honestly and reasonably')

Where members knowingly receive an unlawful dividend:

- The company can recover this sum from them

- The directors may claim an indemnity from the members in respect of their liability

- Members who have received a dividend in such a way cannot bring a derivative action against the directors

Members cannot under any circumstances authorise in general meeting the payment of an unlawful dividend, nor release the directors from their liability.

- *Flitcroft's case 1882*

> *Exam focus.* Question 6 in May 1997 asked about the funds from which dividends could be paid, and the consequences of an illegal dividend.

An error in the accounts leading to the payment of an unlawful dividend may result in the auditors being liable, if they were negligent or guilty of misfeasance.

> *Exam focus.* The rules you have just revised may seem rather dry and remote. It is important, however, to understand *why* they are necessary, ie to protect the creditors' buffer. Most recent papers have included a question on an aspect of capital maintenance.

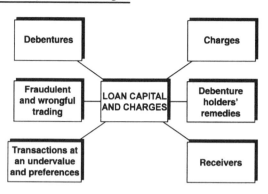

Debentures

Any document stating the terms on which a company has borrowed money is a debenture: s 744. Debentures are usually issued under the common seal. There are three main types.

- A single debenture

- Debentures issued as a series and usually registered

- Debenture stock subscribed to by a large number of lenders. Only this form _requires_ a debenture trust deed, although the others may often incorporate one

Shares and debentures are similar.

- Transferable company securities

- Issue and transfer procedures the same

However, share and debentures are different.

- Shareholder = owner; debentureholder = creditor

- Debentures have priority in liquidation

- Interest on debentures *must* be paid, even out of capital

- No statutory restriction on purchase or redemption of debentures

Charges   *11/96, 11/97, 5/98, 11/98*

A charge over the assets of a company gives a creditor a prior claim over other creditors to payment of his debt out of these assets. Charges may be either *fixed*, which attach to the relevant asset on creation, or *floating*, which only attach on 'crystallisation'.

Priority

Some charges take priority over others. The general rules are as follows.

- Legal (fixed) charges rank according to the order of creation

- If a fixed charge is created *after* a floating charge on the same property, the fixed charge will generally take precedence since the floating charge actually *attaches* to the property after the creation of the fixed charge

- If a legal fixed charge is created after an equitable fixed charge the legal charge will take priority, unless the person to whom the legal charge was given had notice of the existing equitable charge at the time of creation

Registration

Particulars of all charges must be registered with the Registrar of Companies within 21 days.

Failure to register renders the charge void against the liquidator and any person who acquires an interest in property subject to the charge. The loan remains valid but unsecured.

A debentureholder can register the charge if it appears that the company is unlikely to do so.

These proposals have the following problems.

- The charge will be effective from *registration* (not *creation*)

- Subsequent insolvency will render the charge invalid. The relevant periods are as follows.

  - 2 years - floating charge in favour of connected person
  - 1 year - floating charge (unconnected person)
  - 6 months - fixed charge (connected/unconnected)

Comparison

A fixed charge is more satisfactory.

- It gives immediate rights over identified assets, although such assets may not be as easily realisable as assets subject to a floating charge

- Even when a floating charge crystallises it will generally rank behind a fixed charge

---

Exam focus. Part of a November 1996 question required discussion of the rights given by, and limitations of, a floating charge.

Debentureholders' remedies   *11/97, 5/98*

Any debentureholder is a creditor of the company with the normal remedies of an unsecured creditor.

- He may sue the company for debt and seize its property if the judgement for debt is unsatisfied

- He may petition for compulsory liquidation of the company

- He may petition for an administration order

A *secured* debentureholder may enforce the security if the company defaults on payment of interest or repayment of capital.

- He may take possession of the asset subject to the charge and sell it

- He may apply to the court for its transfer to his ownership by a foreclosure order

- He may appoint a receiver of it (the usual first step)

Receivers   *11/97*

Definitions

Administrative receiver - a person appointed under a floating charge to take control of, and to manage the whole or substantially the whole of the company's property.

Receiver - appointed under a fixed charge to take control of specific assets.

Function

- To secure the assets charged

- To collect due rents and profits

- To realise assets (if necessary)

- To pay the net proceeds to the debentureholders (and preferential creditors if necessary)

- Sometimes to act as manager

Appointment

By debentureholders, or their trustee under terms of loan agreement.

Employment contracts

Under the Insolvency Act 1986, a receiver on first appointment has 14 days in which to decide whether to continue employees' contracts. Unless he dismisses them in this time he is deemed to have adopted the contracts and would become personally liable on them.

Following the *Paramount* case (1994) the adoption of employment contracts does not require any formal act. However, the Insolvency Act 1994 restricts liabilities under employment contracts adopted by administrators and administrative receivers to certain 'qualifying liabilities', which must have been incurred after the adoption of the contract.

Exam focus. Question 8 in November 1997 asked about the distinction between fixed and floating charges, the advantages of fixed charges over floating charges and how chargeholders' security could be enforced.

Question 8 in May 1998 asked whether certain arrangements were fixed or floating charges, and about charge registration and debentureholder remedies.

Transactions at an undervalue and preferences

5/95, 11/96

A *transaction at an undervalue* is a gift or transaction in the two years prior to liquidation (or administration) where the company gives consideration of greater value than it received, eg sale at less than full market price.

It is not void if it is in good faith, for the purpose of carrying on the business and there are reasonable grounds for believing it will benefit the company.

The court has power to render *preferences* void.

- A preference is any transaction undertaken with a desire to improve a creditor's position on winding up

- The preference must have been given within six months of liquidation (two years if in favour of a connected person)

Note

Floating charges will be rendered invalid if created within a year (two years to connected persons) and:

- The company was insolvent when the charge was created; and

- No consideration was given in exchange for the charge

If new consideration was given, the charge will be valid to the extent of that consideration.

Fraudulent and wrongful trading 5/95, 11/96

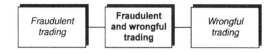

Fraudulent trading

Fraudulent trading is carrying on the business with intent to defraud the creditors when there is no reasonable prospect of their debts being paid.

- There must be 'real dishonesty'

- Only those who take active part are liable
  - *Re Maidstone Building Provisions Ltd 1971*

- Carrying on business can include a single transaction

Those responsible (usually directors) may be liable to make good to company all or some specified part of company's debts. Directors may be disqualified.

Wrongful trading

This is a civil liability introduced because it was difficult to prove fraud. Directors liable in the following cases.

- Directors of insolvent company knew or should have known that there was no reasonable prospect that the company could have avoided going into insolvent liquidation

- Directors did not take sufficient steps to minimise the potential loss to the creditors

Director will be deemed to know if that would have been the conclusion of a reasonably diligent person. The test is therefore objective, requiring hindsight, and it is not easy to predict the outcome of a particular case.

Exam focus. The case law on fraudulent and wrongful trading is still developing and hence is a likely exam topic.

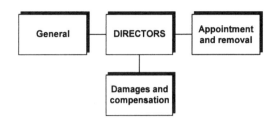

Note. Other topics in Chapter 24 of the Study Text are summarised in the next chapter on powers and duties.

General

Any person who occupies the position of a director is treated as such: s 741. The test is one of function.

A *shadow director* is any person (except a professional advisor) by whose directions the board is accustomed to act (but who is not officially a director).

An *alternate director* is a person appointed by a director to attend board meetings and vote on his behalf.

A *non-executive director* is a director who merely sits on the board, with no additional management duties. If the articles provide for it, a *managing director* may be appointed.

Every company must have at least one director, and for a public company the minimum is two: s 282. There is no statutory maximum.

Appointment and removal   5/98

The method of appointing directors, along with their rotation and co-option is controlled by the articles, allowing a company a wide discretion in the matter.

Provisions in the articles for dismissal of a director are overridden by statute, allowing removal by ordinary resolution with special notice: s 303. The director may require a memorandum to be circulated to members, and has a right to speak at the meeting on the resolution: s 304.

Directors may also be required to vacate office because they have been disqualified; again the grounds may be dictated by the articles, which may override statute in some areas.

Grounds of disqualification under Table A Article 81 include the following.

- Disqualification by the Act or any rule of law

- Ceasing to hold any qualification shares required

- Becoming bankrupt or entering into an arrangement with creditors

- Becoming of unsound mind

- Written resignation

- Absence from board meetings for six consecutive months without leave of absence, if the board resolves that he should be removed

Directors (and other persons) *may* be disqualified from a very wide range of company involvements under the Company Directors Disqualification Act 1986 (CDDA). The grounds are as follows.

- Conviction of an indictable offence in connection with the promotion, formation, management or liquidation of a company or with the receivership or management of a company's property: s 2

- Persistent default in relation to provisions of company legislation: s 3

- Fraudulent trading in the course of a winding up: s 4

- A court order that the person concerned is unfit to be involved in the management of a company: s 8

- Participation in wrongful trading: s10

The court *must* make an order under the CDDA where a person has been a director of a company which became insolvent, and his conduct as a director makes him unfit to be concerned in the management of a company: s 6.

Damages and compensation

A director may be entitled to substantial damages if his service contract is breached.

If there is no service contract he may receive non-contractual compensation, but this is only lawful if:

- Approved in general meeting

- Proper disclosure made to *all* members

> *Exam focus.* The matters discussed in this chapter are factual, and therefore likely to form the basis of a multiple choice question. More complex issues are discussed in the next chapter; these are likely to be the basis of a problem question in Section B of the paper.

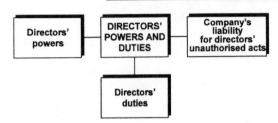

Directors' powers   5/97, 5/98

The powers of directors are defined by the articles. They have a duty to exercise their powers in what they honestly believe to be the best interests of the company, and for the purpose(s) for which the powers are given.

If members do not like the acts of directors, they can remove them under s 303 or change the articles; they cannot retrospectively restrict the directors or take over the company management.

If the articles provide for it, one or more directors may be appointed by the board as managing director.

- He has *apparent* authority to make business contracts on behalf of the company

- His *actual* authority is whatever the board give him

Exam focus. Part of question 7 in May 1997 related to directors' ability to commit the company to guaranteeing the debts of another company.

Question 8 in May 1997 asked about the division of powers between directors and members, Question 8 in November 1998 asked about shareholders exercising control over directors.

Company's liability for directors' unauthorised acts

S/97, S/98

A person who deals with a company through persons who appear to be directors can usually enforce the contract.

- Under the principle in *Royal British Bank v Turquand 1856*; or

- As a result of s 285, which provides that the acts of a director or manager are valid notwithstanding any defects that may afterwards be discovered in his appointment or qualification

- Under s 35 which generally validates *ultra vires* acts, and s 35A which applies to most *intra vires* acts (and is argued to be wider in scope than the *Turquand* principle)

The rule in *Turquand's* case is subject to the following six circumstances where it will *not* apply.

- Where the person dealing with the directors was aware that they were acting without authority

- Where the person who claims against the company is an insider, and has the opportunity of discovering whether the authorisation has been given

- Where there are suspicious circumstances which put the outsider under a duty to inquire and he fails to do so

- Where the necessary authorisation requires the passing of a special resolution which must then be delivered to the registrar for filing

- Where the document is a forgery, unless perhaps it is produced by an agent of the company whose status gives him ostensible authority to issue it

- Where the transaction is so unusual that the third party is put on enquiry whether the purported agent has the powers which he represents himself as having

If the principal (the company) *holds out* a person as its authorised agent, then it is estopped from denying that he is its authorised agent. This is a basic application of the law of agency.

- *Freeman & Lockyer v Buckhurst Park Properties 1964*

Directors' duties

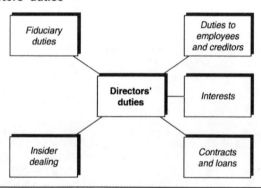

Exam focus. This section is very important as most papers in the last few years have contained a question which related to directors' duties.

Fiduciary duties   *11/95, 5/97, 11/97, 5/98, 11/98*

Directors are said to be in a *fiduciary* position in relation to the company. They owe a number of strictly applied fiduciary duties to the company.

- They must exercise their powers *bona fide* in what they consider to be the best interests of the company

- The powers of directors must only be used for a proper purpose. The transaction is invalid unless the company in general meeting ratifies it

- They must retain their freedom of action and not fetter their discretion by agreeing to vote as some other person may direct. They may represent the interests of, say, a shareholder or debentureholder. This may, however, lead to conflicts of interest which may be difficult to resolve

- The directors must avoid conflicts of duty and personal interest
  - This rule is very strictly applied
    - *Aberdeen Railway Co v Blaikie Bros 1854*
  - It is unnecessary to show that the company has been prejudiced in any way by the conflict of interest

- No personal gain should be made from the position of director without the consent of the company
  - No need to show lack of good faith
    - Need only show that director has made a profit through an opportunity which came to him as a director. The above applies even if the company was unable to take up the opportunity
    - *Regal (Hastings) Ltd v Gulliver 1942*

- If a director benefits from his position (directly or indirectly) he must disclose this and get permission to retain the benefit. Permission can be given by ordinary resolution or by the board (Table A Article 85)

If a breach occurs, the arrangement is voidable, the directors must return profits and make good losses and may be treated as holding the proceeds on constructive trust.

The directors also have a common law duty of *reasonable competence*, the test being applied on the basis of knowledge and experience. Relief is available for directors acting honestly and reasonably.

> *Exam focus.* Both 1997 papers included questions about actions by directors to which fiduciary duties and specific statutory rules were relevant. This overlap often occurs (eg when a director fails to disclose an interest, he may be in breach of the equitable fiduciary duty not to make secret profits and s 317.)

Duties to employees and creditors   5/96

The directors have a duty to, *and* enforceable, by the *company* to consider the interests of employees: s 309. The directors have a duty to the company to consider generally creditors' interests in times of insolvency (*West Mercia Safetyware case*).

> *Exam focus.* A May 1996 question required discussion of director duties towards members, employees and creditors. You should remember that the directors' duties are generally owed to the company (the general body of members).

Interests

A register of the 'notifiable' interests of directors in shares or debentures must be kept with the register of members or at the registered office, and is similarly open to the public.

A 'notifiable interest' in shares or debentures includes direct ownership, and interests through trusts, controlled body corporates or close family.

Contracts and loans   *5/97, 11/97, 11/98*

Under s 317, a director must 'declare the nature of his interest', direct or indirect, in a contract or proposed contract with the company.

Disclosure must be to the first meeting of the directors at which the contract is considered or (if later) the first meeting held after the director becomes interested in the contract. Generally the director must not vote or be reckoned as one of the quorum at the board meeting.

Approval from the shareholders is required under s 320 for any contract by which the company buys from, or sells to, a director property:

- Exceeding £100,000 in value
- Or (if less) 10 per cent of the company's net assets
- Subject to a minimum of £2,000 in value

'Material' interests of directors in contracts with the company must be disclosed in the annual accounts.

Any *service agreement* exceeding five years duration must be approved by the company in general meeting. Without such approval:

- The contract is still valid
- It may be terminated by the company on giving reasonable notice at any time

Members have a statutory right to inspect any director's service agreement which exceeds one year.

S 330 says that a company may not make a loan to a director of itself or of its holding company or enter into any guarantee or provide any security in connection with such a loan.

S 334 says loans may be made up to £5,000 per director. Inter-company loans etc are not prohibited.

There are a number of exceptions.

- Those applying to all companies (expense advances)

- Those only applying to money-lending companies (standard loans and loans to purchase main residence)

The Act refers to 'relevant' companies - these are plc's and companies that are part of a group containing plcs.

In relevant companies, the loan rules also apply to shadow directors and connected persons. There may be criminal liability for breaches.

Insider dealing

Part V of the Criminal Justice Act 1993 contains rules prohibiting insider dealing.

S 52 describes *the offence* as

- Dealing in securities

- While in possession of insider information as an insider

- The securities being price-affected by the information

The legislation covers off-market transactions between or involving 'professional intermediaries' (not just transactions on a designated exchange).

There are various anti-avoidance measures including those relating to encouraging others to deal or the disclosure of information to other parties.

S 55 defines *dealing* as acquiring or disposing of or agreeing to acquire or dispose of relevant securities whether directly through an agent or nominee or a person acting according to direction.

S 54 states that the securities covered by the Act are as follows.

- Shares or stock in the share capital of a company

- Debt securities (eg gilts)

- All forms of warrants, depository receipts, options, futures, contracts for differences based on individual securities or an index

S 56 defines *inside information* as 'price sensitive information' relating to a particular issuer of securities that are price-affected and not to securities generally; it must be specific or precise and, if made public, be likely to have a significant effect on price.

S 57 states that a person has information as an *insider* in the following cases.

- It is (and he knows it is) inside information

- He has it (and knows he has) from an inside source: through being a director, employee or shareholder of an issuer of securities; through access because of employment, office or profession

- If the direct or indirect source is a person within these two previous categories

'Connection' with the issuer need not be shown.

S 58 defines the term *made public*, but not exhaustively, leaving final determination to the court. Information is made public in the following cases.

- It is published under the rules of a regulated market, such as the Stock Exchange

- It is in public records, for example, notices in the *London Gazette*

- It can readily be acquired by those likely to deal

- It is derived from public information

Information may be treated as made public even in the following cases.

- It can only be acquired by exercising diligence or expertise (thus helping analysts to avoid liability)

- It is communicated only to a section of the public (thus protecting the 'brokers' lunch' where a company informs only selected City sources of important information)

- It can be acquired only by observation

- It is communicated only on payment of a fee or is published only outside the UK

S 53 gives a *general defence* where the individual concerned can show any of the following.

- He did not expect there to be a profit or avoidance of loss

- He had reasonable grounds to believe that the information had been disclosed widely

- He would have done what he did even if he had not had the information, for example where securities are sold to pay a pressing debt

Defences to disclosure of information by an individual are that:

- He did not expect any person to deal

- Although dealing was expected, profit or avoidance of loss was not

Special defences are given in Schedule 1 and are generally available to market makers, those in possession of marketing information and those engaged in a price stabilisation exercise.

Maximum *penalties* given by s 61 are seven years' imprisonment and/or an unlimited fine. Contracts remain valid and enforceable at civil law.

Exam focus. The above rules on insider dealing are likely to come up in an exam soon.

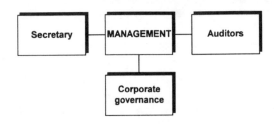

Secretary

Every company must have a secretary. The company secretary may not also be the sole director.

In a public company s 286 imposes a duty on directors to satisfy themselves that the person appointed as secretary can adequately fulfil the position. The specific requirements are:

- A qualified accountant

- A barrister or solicitor

- Person who has been company secretary in a plc for 3 out of the last 5 years

- A person who was company secretary on 22 December 1980

- A chartered secretary

- Any other person who appears to be capable by virtue of any other position held

Secretaries can bind the company to the extent of their 'apparent authority'. This usually means contracts of an administrative nature only.

- *Panorama v Fidelis Furnishing Fabrics Ltd 1971*

> *Exam focus.* Question 7(c) in November 1998 asked about a company secretary's powers and duties.

Auditors

11/95

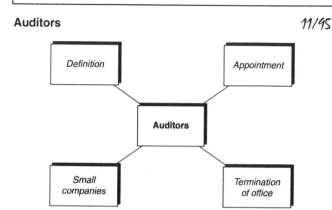

Definition

An audit is an independent examination and expression of opinion upon the financial statements of an enterprise.

The audit report may be unqualified or qualified.

This relates to whether, in the auditors' opinion, the accounts give a true and fair view of the company's financial statements.

Appointment

Every company (except certain small companies) must appoint auditors: s 389.

The appointment is made by:

- (Normally) members in AGM where accounts are laid

- Directors or members in general meeting for first auditors or to fill casual vacancy

- Failing the above by Secretary of State

Termination of office

- Removal by ordinary resolution with special notice, auditors having right to:
  o Circularise a written statement to members
  o Speak in general meeting

- Resignation by notice in writing to registered office
  o Auditors must submit written statement to company
  o Auditors can requisition an EGM

- Auditors do not seek re-election
  o Auditors must submit written statement to company
  o Prevents auditors keeping suspicions secret

Small companies

- A company is totally exempt from audit if turnover $\leq$ £350,000 and the balance sheet total $\leq$ £1.4m

- Exemptions do not apply to:
  o Public companies
  o Banking/insurance companies
  o Companies subject to statute-based regime

Shareholders holding $\geq$ 10% of capital can veto exemption.

Exam focus. The November 1995 exam had, as a six mark part of a question, the requirement to discuss whether all companies require an audit.

Corporate governance

The corporate governance codes are primarily aimed at listed companies, although all companies are encouraged to comply. Listed companies must state whether they have complied with the principles and provisions of the Stock Exchange Code that combines the three reports listed below.

Cadbury Report

The report stated that the major elements of corporate governance were the board of directors, shareholders and auditors.

Aspects of corporate governance covered by the report included role and structure of board of directors, appointment and independence of non-executive directors, determination of executive directors' remuneration and controls.

Greenbury Report

This focused on remuneration, requiring listed companies to set up a remuneration committee consisting of non-executive directors, and to report on remuneration policy and details of individual directors' remuneration packages.

Hampel Report

This report stressed the importance of flexibility and that corporate governance codes should be guidelines rather than prescriptive rules. The major areas covered were directors, directors' remuneration, shareholders and the AGM, and accountability and audit.

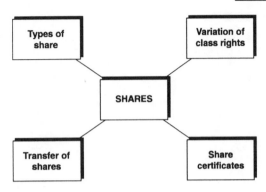

Types of share

A share is the interest of a shareholder in the company.

- The share must be paid for

- It gives a proportionate entitlement to dividends, votes and any return of capital

- It is a form of bargain between shareholders which underlies such principles as majority control and minority protection

- The main types of share are ordinary shares and preference shares.

Ordinary shares

These are the majority of shares. They give entitlement to dividends and normally a full right to vote.

Preference shares

Preference shareholders have the right to receive dividend at specified rate before any other dividends are declared. Common types include the following.

- *Cumulative:* preference shares are assumed to be cumulative. Unpaid dividend is carried forward and paid before any other dividends when a dividend is finally declared

- *Non-cumulative:* no accumulation right

- *Participating:* basic dividend plus right to share in surplus profits after ordinary shares have been paid. This right must be expressly stated

- *Redeemable:* company has right of redemption

- *Priority on liquidation*

Variation of class rights

Class rights are rights attaching to a particular class of share (eg right to a preference dividend). They are usually defined in the memorandum/articles. A summary of the s 125 requirements is contained in the following table.

Class rights	Variation procedure	Legal requirement
Memo	None	All members
Arts	None	75% of class in writing *or* extraordinary resolution of class
Memo	Memo	Follow procedure
Arts	Arts	given

An alteration in the variation procedure is a variation of class rights.

Protection for minorities in a variation of class rights is available: s 127.

The following are *not* variations of class rights:

- Issue of shares to non-members of class
  - *White v Bristol Aeroplane Co Ltd 1953*
- Subdivision of shares of another class and thus increasing voting rights of that class
  - *Greenhalgh v Arderne Cinemas Ltd 1946*
- Return of capital to preference shareholders
  - *House of Fraser plc v ACGE Investments Ltd 1987*
- Creation and issue of new class of preference shares
  - *Re John Smith's Tadcaster Brewery Co Ltd 1953*

Share certificates

S 185 states that they must be issued within two months of allotment or transfer.

A share certificate is *prima facie* evidence of title but membership is determined by entries in the register of members: s 186.

Companies will be liable to persons who rely on certificates which are wrongly issued...

- *Re Bahia and San Francisco Railway 1868*

...unless the person obtaining the certificate is using a forged transfer and is therefore estopped from claiming (even if that person is an innocent victim of the forgery).

Most plc's insure against the liability arising from accepting a forged transfer.

Transfer of shares

Mechanics

The diagram below shows the procedure when the whole shareholding is transferred.

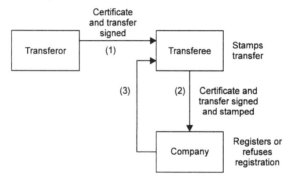

The diagram below shows the certification procedure, appropriate on transfer of part of a shareholding.

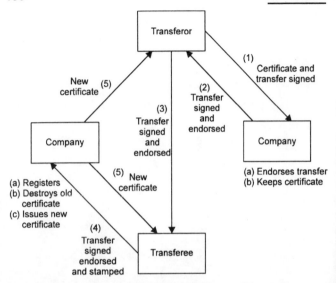

Exam focus. To help you remember these rules, look at the diagram once a day in the week before the exam. Aspects of the procedure may be tested as part of a longer question or as a multiple choice question.

Note the following.

- Certification merely means
  - *Prima facie* title
  - Certificate lodged with company

- Where person relies on certification, the company will be liable if it has been negligent

Directors' power of veto

Directors may have a general or specific power to refuse to transfer shares.

- The power must be exercised by a positive (*bona fide*) decision at a board meeting
  - *Re Hackney Pavilion Ltd 1924*

- The power of veto exists only for a reasonable time. Notice of refusal must be given within two months of the presentation of the transfer

- Directors do not have to give reasons for refusal unless the articles say otherwise

- Remedy is rectification of register

Compulsory transfer

Power may be given to directors to compel a member to transfer his shares on certain grounds. This power must be exercised in good faith and for the company's benefit.

- *Borland's Trustee v Steel Bros 1901*

Forfeiture of shares

If a shareholder defaults in the payment of calls the company may, if the articles so provide, forfeit his shares.

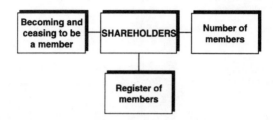

Becoming and ceasing to be a member

A member of a company is a person who:

- Has agreed to be a member
- Whose name has been entered in the register of members

Subscribers to the memorandum are the company's initial shareholders.

A person ceases to be a member in the following circumstances.

- He transfers all his shares to another person and the transfer is registered
- He dies

Number of members   5/95

Public companies: minimum number is 2.

Private companies: may be formed and operate with only one member. The following points apply.

- Sole member/director may not also be the secretary
- Register of members must state that the company has only one member

- Sole member keeps limited liability

- Only one member need subscribe to the memorandum of association

- Resolutions must be evidenced in writing; contracts between sole member and company must be in writing

- Articles amended to allow quorum of one at meetings

- Written record of decisions made by the sole member must be provided to the company

> *Exam focus.* Part of a question on the May 1995 paper required candidates to discuss whether a private company needed more than one member.

Register of members

Every company must keep a *register of members* and must enter in it the following details.

- Name and address of each member
- Class to which he belongs
- Amount paid/considered as paid on shares held
- Number of shares held by each member
- Date of becoming and ceasing to be a member

Any member of the public may inspect the register of members during business hours.

The register may be located:

- At the registered office
- At the place where it is made up

Entry in the register is *prima facie* evidence of membership.

A company will not make a note of *beneficial* ownership. The company deals with the registered holder who is the *legal* owner of the shares.

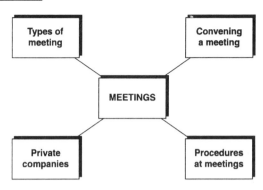

Types of meeting

There are two types of general meeting

- Annual general meeting
- Extraordinary general meeting

Every company must hold an AGM every calendar year, with not more than fifteen months elapsing between each. (A private company can pass an elective resolution dispensing with this rule.)

On default, a member may apply to the DTI.

At least 21 days' notice of an AGM must be given, in writing and in accordance with the articles.

An extraordinary general meeting may be convened at any time:

- By the directors; or
- On the requisition of the members if they constitute one-tenth of the paid up share capital carrying voting rights

An EGM may also be called by the following.

- The Court
- An auditor wishing to give reasons for his resignation

In the case of a public company, the directors must call an EGM if the net assets of the company fall to half the amount of its called up share capital.

Convening a meeting

In order to make valid and binding decisions, a meeting must be properly convened.

- It must be called by a competent person or authority

- The notice must be issued to members in advance of the meeting so as to give them 14 to 21 days 'clear notice' of the meeting

- The notice must be sent to every person entitled to receive it; it need not be sent to any member whose shares do not give him a right to attend and vote

- The notice must include any information reasonably necessary to enable shareholders to know in advance what is to be done

The period of notice for an AGM (or an EGM at which a special resolution is to be proposed) is 21 days. In any other case the standard period is 14 days.

In most circumstances, a prescribed number of members can waive this period should they so wish.

Where *special notice* to the company of the intention to propose a resolution is required, the period is 28 days. Where the necessary number of members require a resolution to be included in the notice of the meeting, a requisition must be delivered to the company at least six weeks in advance of the meeting.

In the case of a special or extraordinary resolution, the notice must set out the text of the resolution in full. Where an ordinary resolution is not routine, setting out the full text avoids disputes.

As a general principle, there must be at least two persons present to constitute a meeting - either in person or by proxy. There are limited exceptions to this rule.

- Class meeting where one person holds all the shares of the class

- Single member private company

Meetings which become inquorate during their proceedings must generally be adjourned, although some older model articles do not include this provision.

The right to appoint a proxy to attend and vote on a member's behalf is statutory: s 372. Proxies appointed by individual members cannot vote on a show of hands, whereas a representative appointed by a corporate member can; both can vote on a poll.

Procedures at meetings   11/96

A meeting can pass three types of resolution.

- An ordinary resolution, carried by a simple majority of votes cast and requiring 14 days notice

- An extraordinary resolution, carried by a 75 per cent majority of votes cast and requiring 14 days notice

- A special resolution, requiring a 75 per cent majority of votes cast and 21 days notice

> *Exam focus.* The most common type of company law MCQ on this paper has been to ask what type of resolution is required to authorise a particular action.

The meeting should have a chairman, who regulates the debate.

- He has a limited inherent power to adjourn, but must do so if the meeting so directs him

- He can refuse amendments, although a motion passed in its original form when an amendment to it has been wrongly rejected will be invalid if challenged

- If voting is by a show of hands, the chairman's decision is deemed to be conclusive but it can be challenged if it is fraudulent or manifestly wrong

There is a common-law right to demand a poll. The articles may lay down the conditions under which a poll may be demanded, but only within very tight guidelines.

Note that under the *assent principle* unanimous assent by those entitled to vote is binding but in most cases, however, proceedings of an improperly constituted meeting are invalid.

Private companies   *11/96*

Special concessions, introduced by CA 89, apply to private companies.

Elective resolutions

- Can be used for five purposes:
  - Dispense with holding AGM
  - Dispense with annual approval of accounts
  - Dispense with annual appointment of auditors

- o Reduce majority required to waive notice for EGM from 95% to 90%
- o Disapply the five year maximum for a director's authority to allot shares

- Can be revoked by ordinary resolution

Written resolutions

- This concession enables the passing of any resolution by obtaining the signature of all members

- It should be sent to the auditors at or before signature. Failure to do this will *not* invalidate the resolution

- It cannot be used to pass ordinary resolutions requiring special notice

Single member private companies   5/95

- Sole member must provide company with a written record of any decision which could have been taken in general meeting

- Must have AGM unless opted out by elective resolution

- May conduct business by written resolution

Exam focus. The November 1996 exam required a list of the different types of resolution a company could pass, and examples of each.

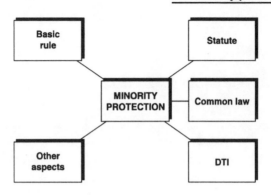

Basic rule

'The proper plaintiff for wrongs done to a company is the company itself, acting through its majority shareholders.'

- *Foss v Harbottle 1853*

Thus decisions made or ratified by the majority cannot be disputed by the minority. This prevents numerous minor actions or a case being brought by the minority and then ratified by the company.

Statute   *5/97, 5/98, 11/98*

Application can be made to the court by any member on the grounds that the company's affairs are being, have been or will be conducted in a manner unfairly prejudicial to him.

The Companies Act 1989 amended s 459 so that it also covers conduct which is unfairly prejudicial to the interests of the 'members generally'.

Examples of conduct that may be unfairly prejudicial include:

- Exclusion and removal from board
  - *Re Bird Precision Bellows 1985*

- Improper allotment of shares
  - *Re D R Chemicals 1989*

- Failure to call a meeting
  - *Re McGuinness and Another 1988*

- Making an inaccurate statement to shareholders
  - *Re A Company 1986*

- Diversion of assets for personal benefit
  - *Re London School of Electronics 1985*

- Payment of excessive directors' bonuses
  - *Re Cumana 1986*

- Prolonged payment of low dividends

Application can also be made by persons who are not members.

- The Secretary of State following a DTI report
- Persons whose share transfers have not been registered

The court has four powers.

- Regulate the conduct of the company's affairs in the future

- Require the company to stop the act being complained about

- Authorise civil proceedings

- Provide for the purchase of shares by members of the company

- o   *SCWS v Meyer 1958* - shares are valued at their pre-prejudice price

- *Re Bird Precision Bellows 1985* - shares are valued as though they were part of a majority holding

---

Exam focus. The examiner has stated that discussion of s 459 will invariably form part of any answer on shareholders' rights.

Common law   5/97

There are a number of *common law* exceptions where an individual member may bring an action.

- The act is illegal

- The act has been sanctioned by a simple majority when a special resolution is required

- The personal rights of a member have been infringed
  - o   *Pender v Lushington 1877*

- The majority are committing a fraud on the minority
  - o   *Cook v Deeks 1916*

- Directors have benefited at the expense of the company through their own negligence
  - o   *Daniels v Daniels 1977* (but note *Pavlides v Jensen 1956*)

- The court will take account of the *intention* of the majority when deciding whether their actions are legitimate
  - o   *Clemens v Clemens Bros Ltd 1976*

Types of action

- Personal - a member sues on his own behalf

- Representative - a member sues on behalf of a group of members

- Derivative - a member sues on behalf of the company

DTI

The DTI has statutory power to appoint an inspector (or joint inspectors) as follows.

- To investigate the affairs of a company

- To investigate the ownership of a company

- To investigate suspected infringement by directors of statutory rules relating to their interests or dealings in options over shares or debentures of their company

- To investigate suspected insider dealing: s 177 FSA

The DTI also has a statutory power to require a company or its officers to produce to the DTI documents and to provide an explanation of any of them. The power extends to any person who is not an officer but who appears to have company documents in his possession.

The DTI may in its discretion appoint inspectors to investigate the affairs of a company in any of the following situations.

- The company itself applies

- Application is made by members who are not less than 200 in number or who hold at least one tenth of the issued shares

- The DTI considers that the affairs of the company have been conducted

    o In a fraudulent or unlawful manner (or that it was formed for a fraudulent or unlawful purpose) o In a manner unfairly prejudicial to some part of its members

o Members have not been given all the information with respect to its affairs which they might reasonably expect

Other aspects

Minorities also have statutory rights in the following situations.

● Variation of class rights

● Alteration of objects (15% shareholders)

● Requisition a meeting

● Requisition company to give notice of members' resolutions to AGM (1/20 voting rights)

● Public company converted to private - 5% or 50 members may object

● Prevent purchase of own shares or financial assistance (10% shareholders)

● Full notice for AGM

● Full notice for special resolution (5%)

● Demand a poll (10% or 5 members)

● Compulsory winding-up of company on just and equitable grounds

● Require DTI investigation

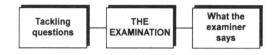

Tackling questions

Here is an approach to tackling law questions.

- Read the question requirements

- Read the question carefully with the requirements in mind. Make notes if it helps

- Plan your answer

- State the legal principles involved, supporting your answer with case law, statute and examples where appropriate

- Apply the law to the problem in the question. There is not always a 'right' or 'wrong' answer and credit is given for understanding the law and applying it

What the examiner says

The following comments have been made by the examiner since the present syllabus has been in place. Bear them in mind!

- Most scripts are reasonably good. Few are excellent

- Many candidates just say 'guilty' or 'not guilty', 'liable' or 'not liable'. Candidates must give reasons for their answers and explain the legal principles which they are applying

- Exam technique and up-to-date knowledge are vital